C000278064

A GUIDE TO NEW PO

How to do politics in the 21st century

Nick Silver is a founder/director of Radix. Nick is Chairman of Climate Bonds Initiative and CEO of Callund Consulting Limited. He is a visiting fellow at City University and Anglia Ruskin University. Nick's recent book *Finance, Society and Sustainability* is published by Palgrave McMillan.

Zoe Hodge is a research fellow at Radix.

Tim Bale is Professor of Politics at Queen Mary University of London. In 2008 he won the Political Studies Association's Bernard Crick Prize for Outstanding Teaching. In 2011 he received the W.J.M. Mackenzie prize for his book The Conservative Party from Thatcher to Cameron. The 4th edition of his textbook on European Politics was published in 2017.

Acknowledgments

We would like to thank Joe Zammit-Lucia, David Boyle, Magda Polan, Guy de Selliers, Corrado Polli, Koen Vossen, Nicholas Firzli, Antònia Casellas, Tim Bale and Nick Tyrone for their invaluable help.

About Radix

Radix is a cross-party think thank for the radical centre. Our goal is a sustainable society where all citizens can live securely with dignity, are active participants in society and are free to pursue their own interpretation of the good life. We aim to achieve this by re-imagining our system of political economy and the way our institutions function by using contemporary ideas and technologies.

A Guide to New Political Movements

Movements

How to do politics in the

21st century

Nick Silver & Zoe Hodge

Foreword by

Tim Bale

www.radix.org.uk

This edition published in 2019 by:
Radix Group Ltd. 76, Vincent Square, London SW1
www.radix.org.uk © Radix

A Kindle edition is also available.

The moral right of Nick Silver and Zoe Hodge to be identified
as the author of this work has been asserted in accordance
with the Copyright, Designs and Patents Acts of 1988.

ISBN (print edition) 978-1-912880-05-8

Printed by CPI Group (UK) Ltd, Croydon CR0 4YY

Contents

Foreword

Remember *Borgen* – the hit drama from Denmark about the political and personal travails of every liberal-progressive's favourite female politician, Birgitte Nyborg?

Brilliant wasn't it? Well, Series One and Two anyway. Series Three didn't quite measure up. You might recall it wasn't so much about the parliamentary cut and thrust of coalition government any more. Instead, it was about Birgitte starting a political party from scratch. And it was totally unrealistic.

Or was it?

True, everything – funding, membership, manifesto – seemed to fall into place a little too rapidly. Sure, there were some serious internal tensions, a cancer scare, a red scare, and more than a betrayal or two. Yet, in the space of a few short months (or maybe even weeks), Birgitte's New Democrats defy the polls to beat her old outfit, the centrist Moderate Party in a snap general election. She herself then defies expectations by becoming Foreign Secretary in a coalition that includes the anti-immigration Freedom Party.

But given what we've seen across a pretty wide range of democracies recently, and as detailed in the pages that follow, is this really that hard to believe? With traditional party systems and the established parties that dominated them for years failing to keep pace with a raft of profound social, cultural and economic changes – changes that have effectively

> Traditional parties have, for years, failed to keep pace with profound social, cultural and economic changes

fractured familiar bases of support and created a less tribal, more consumerist electorate – plenty of space has opened up for potential alternatives.

Just as importantly, the rise of 24/7 multi-channel and social media has made it possible for those alternatives to exploit a seemingly insatiable public demand for the novel, the spectacular and the hyperbolic. It has allowed them to bypass the more staid, more regulated, and more balanced media that in times past would have effectively obliged potential supporters to listen to different points of view, if not necessarily to reason.

Is there an off-the-shelf recipe that existing or aspiring new political parties can follow?

Given all this, is there some off-the-shelf recipe for success that aspiring new entrants can follow? Well, if we look at the examples contained within this book – from a range of countries (Italy, France, Spain, and Canada) and professing a range of ideologies and none – it would certainly seem so. Three things appear to be particularly important.

First, charismatic leadership by someone who can convincingly portray themselves as an outsider would seem to be essential, not least because he or she needs somehow to embody the differences between the new party and the 'more of the same' on offer from politicians who look tired, unrepresentative, compromised, and even corrupt, by comparison. Members (often loosely attached) and voters are especially attracted by the chance that, finally, something may actually change.

Second, policies matter, but not as much as we might assume. Process, as well as leadership, is apparently just as important. The emphasis is on new, often digital, methods of consulting supporters (and, inasmuch as they exist in any formal way in these parties, members) in order to arrive at consensual and supposedly common sense, yet innovative solutions to problems that established parties have allowed to fester for years, in hock as they are to vested interests of various hues.

Thirdly, communication – particularly targeted communication based on harvesting data and involving some seriously savvy playing of the 21st century media game – is also all important. One thing successful new parties seem to have in common is the ability to use digital platforms to mobilise potential supporters – many of whom may previously have given up on politics or had never even considered it an option – to move from online, initially passive support, to the offline, 'in real life' activity that helps win seats in parliament.

Of course, as the book reveals, not everything in the new parties' gardens is rosy. For one thing, their claims to be democratic require an enormous pinch of salt. Their determined rejection of intermediate layers of governance that might interfere in the supposedly direct relationship between charismatic leaders and relatively atomised supporters means that, in reality, the former rather than the latter are very much in charge. Fine, and to some extent understandable, in opposition, perhaps. But in government, when things really begin to count, that's rather more problematic.

For another, although the book plays it down, there is more than simply a touch of populism about these parties. Many observers would even suggest, in fact, that the p-word is the key to understanding their appeal and their *modus operandi* – indeed, maybe, in one or two cases (Italy's Five Star comes immediately to mind in this respect), populism is their very essence. For some observers, this isn't necessarily a bad thing. For others, it represents a clear and present danger to a tried and tested system of representative democracy. Look what happened, they point out, when a populist insurgency in the form of UKIP persuaded David Cameron to hold a referendum on the UK's membership of the EU.

Which brings us, lastly, to one of the book's most interesting questions: could it happen in the UK and other countries that use a first-past-the post system rather than a system of proportional representation? Well, as we've just seen, in some senses it already has. As the book itself notes, citing UKIP and the SDP's role in catalysing New Labour, new parties can significantly influence events, even if they don't win formal power. And in any case, the book observes, we mustn't ignore the possibility that old parties – Justin Trudeau's Canadian Liberals being the best example – can very effectively re-fashion themselves as new.

> The UK's political system may well be less resistant to the shock of the new than many of us imagine

The UK's electoral system is a cruel master but, as Labour's replacement of the Liberals as the main opposition to the Tories in the early twentieth century shows, it is not an utterly impossible obstacle to overcome. If Brexit blows apart traditional political identities, and if its poor handling by both main parties ends up alienating even their core supporters, we may well find the UK's political system is rather less resistant to the shock of the new than many of us imagine.

Tim Bale
Professor of Politics
Queen Mary University of London

1

Overview

The emergence of new, or non-traditional parties has coincided with the collapse of incumbent parties in many countries. This book is the result of a detailed analysis on four parties, three new and one new/old, analysing how they have emerged, organised themselves and achieved electoral success. Radix has also commissioned five European writers to write short pieces on the rise of new parties in their countries.

The analysis provides insight into how a new party can organise itself, or how an old party can re-invent itself to best harness new technologies in a changed political environment.

The new parties combine policies which traditional parties would not; they are organised differently to traditional parties, they are led by people who would not be in charge of traditional parties and who say things that traditional politicians wouldn't. They pride themselves on being outsiders, setting themselves apart from incumbent elites. The parties portray themselves as democracies opposed to corporatism and the vested interests that have captured government and the old, incumbent parties.

> New parties do and say things that traditional parties would not

This book is not intended to be an advocate for any of the new political parties. In fact, we believe that many of their political platforms are deeply flawed and contradictory. But then again, new parties may not have a monopoly on people within their ranks pushing for flawed and contradictory policies.

The Birth of the New

These new, and new/old parties, have emerged because of long-term socio-economic developments, dramatic changes in the media landscape, technology, use of data, and an erosion of the social contract. The broad interest groups that make up the voting population has radically changed and does not reflect the coalitions represented by traditional parties.

> Successful new parties have managed to embody a spirit of insurgency and challenge to the status quo

A key event was the 2008 financial crisis and its aftermath which fatally eroded the social contract. Subsequently, we are seeing the collapse of the centre right and left parties which have dominated governments since the war in many countries.

New parties have harnessed technology to engage with people. The crisis has led to further support for entrenched and extreme ideologies, but it has also allowed for the political rulebook to be re-written.

Successful new or new/old parties have managed to embody a spirit of insurgency and challenge to the status quo. Specifically, they have the following in common:

- Parties all have a *charismatic leader* who portrays him/herself, and is seen, as an outsider

- The party, movement or leader has a *critical mass of followers* who can form the basis of the party membership

- Under-represented *coalitions of voters* often identify with the parties, especially people who don't usually vote

- Supporters have been *mobilised* through varied but unconventional use of modern and traditional media

- The parties have *recruited* supporters from other parties and people new to politics

- Parties collect and analyse *data* to tailor image and accurately target voters

- Social media facilitates effective *physical meetings*

Background conditions

- Establishment parties appear tired, ineffective, out of touch, compromised, corrupt, unrepresentative and only interested in preserving their power

- The parties have all managed to develop and disseminate a *successful message* along the lines of things are not right, we are different, we/you can change things

- The *image* that these new parties create as insurgents who oppose the status quo and who involve people on a continuous basis is of crucial importance. The policies that emerge from that are secondary to the success of the parties.

A process, not a party

A new party derives its energy and purpose from the process of creating itself, not governing or active politics. Social media is used to create, tailor and disseminate an image for the party embodied in the party leader. It is also

> A new party derives its energy from the process of creating itself, not governing or active politics

used to mobilise followers: making them active and engaged participants in the party. The structure of new parties can be thought of as a process rather than a traditional hierarchical party. The process works irrespective of the party's policies or ideological origins.

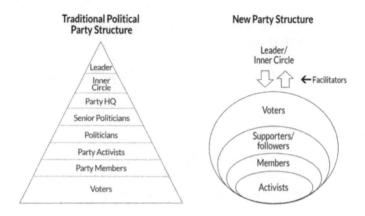

The followers are a social or political network, with some followers acting like hubs, with multiple connections. We have identified four stages of the new party process:

1. Establish a *critical mass* of followers: these can be the followers of a leader or existing party, or arise out of a movement, meetings or protests.

2. Lines of *constant, two-way communication* are established between the leader and the followers to establish a bond, create a conversation or stream of information.

3. *Mobilisation of followers* using social media and technology to organise *meaningful physical interactions* between followers and between followers and the public. These interactions occur on a regular basis – not just around election time. They have the triple purpose of converting supporters into activists,

collecting data and information from the meetings and facilitating interaction between activists and the wider public.

4. A key function of this interaction is for the party and leader to *create and tailor their image* and accurately disseminate their message, which is achieved using the already established communication channels.

Characteristics of new parties

- *The Outsiders v The Elite*: All the parties studied display traits associated with populism, arguing that the system is run by the elites for the elites, the people no longer count and are not listed to. The parties address the wishes of sections of the population, often disaffected, willing to vote for a new alternative that apparently addresses their wishes.

- The *rejection of ideology* is a key part of the messaging of these new parties. The new parties portray themselves as being different from old parties in that they reject the notion of having an ideology at all – they have practical, common sense solutions, even policies developed by the voters themselves.

- The *leader as substitute for ideology*: one apparent contradiction of this democratic wave is that all four parties have dominating charismatic leaders. The leader becomes the defining feature of the party. The political alliances of older parties to civil organisations does not exist. Members, and by extension, voters have an apparent direct link with the leader.

Flaws in the Machine

The process which has brought about spectacular election success for new parties may contain the seeds of their ultimate decline, which becomes manifest once they achieve political power. These problems boil down to too much concentration of power (either in the leader and his inner circle, or with the controller of the party's platform), opacity of decision-making process, lack of expert oversight of party's policies and inability to incorporate dissenting views.

The streamlined structure of the party can leave little checks on power or formal mechanisms for party members to challenge the leadership. The new party process is lacking a middle tier of career politicians.

For example, *République En Marche* and the *Canadian Liberals* are being run by a small coterie of the leader plus his trusted advisors, with clever use of technology to appear close to the people. In contrast, Five Star are seen as being too democratic, with policies developed by supporters which are inconsistent and often unrealistic.

> The process that brings about electoral success contains the seeds of ultimate demise

It remains to be seen whether these new parties are ephemeral phenomena. Now that they are in power, will they turn themselves into more traditional parties or will they disappear as quickly as they emerged? Will a second wave of new parties emerge, or will the traditional parties return, maybe adopting some of the techniques of the new parties?

The key challenge for a new party is to combine the energy and idealism that went into its creation with political experience and governance skills to turn itself into a successful government and long-lasting political force.

Then again, these new movements are not unique in facing existential decline once they enter government. As the Liberal Democrats in the UK, the Labour Party in the Netherlands, the FDP and the SDP in Germany, and others have shown, entering into coalition government with others can be fatal or near fatal even for long-established, traditional parties. Conversely, *La Lega* in Italy has soared in popularity once it took the reins of government and Matteo Salvini, its highly effective and charismatic leader, used the platform of Deputy Prime Minister to overshadow the Five Star Movement.

Cracking the UK

The factors that gave rise to new parties in Europe and other countries exist in abundance in Britain; it has experienced the same social and economic trends as other European countries, and the impact of the financial crisis was especially pronounced. Following the financial crisis and with the shambles of Brexit, the perceived competence of the traditional political parties is at an all-time low.

An obvious barrier in the UK is the first-past-the-post (FPTP) voting system which dis-favours smaller parties whose vote is relatively evenly spread. Our analysis is that there is a threshold over which there is a non-linear relationship between votes and seats (see graph next page).

If a new party could surmount a 26-30 per cent threshold, FPTP would work in its favour and it would swallow up the votes of the previous second party. In Europe, many new parties have crossed this threshold.

> First-past-the-post system would favour any party that surmounts the 26-30% share of vote threshold

The FPTP voting system favours regional parties and there are non-general election opportunities which are not FPTP which could be captured by a party targeted at these localities. Alternatively, a new party may not necessarily have the objective of winning a general election, but of changing the political landscape, as happened with the Social Democratic Party (SDP) and UK Independence Party (UKIP).

UK parties have significant success if they can crack the 26-30% threshold

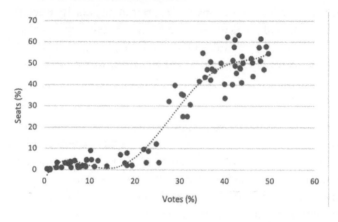

2

Birth of the new

Political revolutions are occurring in many parts of the world. Trump and Macron - non-politicians - have become Presidents of two of the world's largest economies. The populist Five Star movement, fronted by comedian Beppe Grillo until it came to power, is in government in Italy. Andrej Babiš, a businessman and entrepreneur, became Prime Minister of the Czech Republic only three years after entering politics. Syriza are in government in Greece. AfD and the Greens now take a significant share of the vote in Germany. Hungary and Poland are ruled by populist and illiberal parties. In emerging market democracies, Brazil has recently installed a far-right President in Jair Bolsonaro and Mexico, a far-left President in Andres Lopez Obrador. Pakistan is now ruled by former cricket captain Imran Kahn.

Characterising the rise of new parties as mere 'populism' is only partially true

These revolutions are characterised as the rise of populism, but this is only partially true. What we are seeing is the emergence of new, or non-traditional parties. These parties do not necessarily have new ideas, but they often combine policies which traditional parties would not normally espouse; they are organised differently to traditional parties; they are led by people who would not be in charge of traditional parties, who say things that traditional politicians wouldn't. These parties pride themselves on being outsiders in opposition to incumbent elites.

The new parties represent a wide range of political viewpoints and methods of coming to power, some well thought through and some accidental. Some of these parties are not even new but are old parties which have been captured by new leaders, or members, or were marginal for years and are now achieving electoral success – these are referred to as new/old parties in the book.

We have carried out a detailed analysis of four parties, three new and one new/old, analysing how they have arisen and in particular how they have organised themselves and achieved electoral success. Radix has also commissioned five European writers to write short pieces on the rise of new parties in their countries. The reader will find these presented in the Annex, with pieces on France, the Netherlands, Poland, Spain and Italy. The political leanings of the parties have deliberately been kept varied. The analysis is synthesised into common themes.

New and new/old parties have arisen because of long-term changes in socio-economic structures, the change in the media landscape, technology, use of data, and an erosion of the social contract following the 2008 financial crisis, or just dissatisfaction with the status quo and the stalling of political discourse.

This book is written from a UK perspective, the purpose of the analysis is to provide insight into how a new party could organise itself to make use of new opportunities, or what an old party would need to do to re-invent itself. The book also looks at some of the pitfalls and weaknesses of these new parties and ends by discussing whether a new or new/old party could succeed in the UK.

This book is not an advocate for any of the new political parties, in fact we believe that many of their political platforms are deeply flawed and contradictory. Tensions within the structure of these parties are becoming manifest as the parties have achieved power. But in this they are not alone.

As the Liberal Democrats in the UK, the Labour Party in the Netherlands, the FDP and the SDP in Germany, and others have shown, entering into coalition government with others can be fatal or near fatal even for long-established, traditional parties. Conversely, *La Lega* in Italy has soared in popularity once it took the reins of government and Matteo Salvini, its highly effective and charismatic leader, used the platform of Deputy Prime Minister to overshadow the Five Star Movement.

View from Britain

There has been a great deal of media speculation about the prospect of a new centre party in the UK, given the divergence to the left and right of the two main political parties, and the general mess both seem to be in, the ineffectiveness of the Liberal Democrats, half of the population that voted "Remain" being unrepresented on the major issue of the day by the two main parties, and the general perceived disaffection of the British public with the main political parties.

Whilst in many countries in Europe, new parties have been spectacularly successful, there has also been a great deal of media comment that "it couldn't happen here", mainly because the first-past-the-post (FTPT) voting system doesn't favour new parties, and the experience of the Social Democratic Party (SDP) in the 1980s has acted as a cautionary warning to potential break-outs from existing parties.

Can replicating new parties in other countries be translated into success in the UK, given the uniquely British barrier of FPTP, along with other barriers that are common amongst countries?

New parties past in the UK

Despite the FTPT voting system, new parties have emerged in Britain, and although most have had limited success in terms of Parliamentary seats, the more successful ones have left a mark on British politics and society. First and foremost was the Labour Party, formed in 1900. By the 1920s, it was already the major opposition party, replacing the Liberals. It has subsequently been in power a number of times, with variable success.

The British Union of Fascists (BUF) was formed in 1932, out of the ashes of Sir Oswald Mosley's previous venture, the New Party. Though the BUF gained considerable support, fortunately the British public rejected its ideology and pro-Nazi stance in the run up to the Second World War.

The Social Democratic Party (SDP) was established when four leading figures split from the Labour Party in 1981, which they felt was becoming irredeemably left-wing. After forming an alliance with the Liberal Party, they were for a time immensely popular, at one stage leading the opinion polls. But Margaret Thatcher's Conservatives received a massive popularity boost from the Falklands War, and in the 1983 election, the Alliance came third, with a very credible 25 per cent of the vote, though this did not translate into an equivalent proportion of seats in Parliament.

Most of the party eventually merged with the Liberals in 1988. But the impact of the SDP on British politics was probably greater via their influence on Labour, and possibly the Conservatives as well – the emergence of New Labour under Tony Blair (which itself could be seen as a new/old party), and the Conservative Government under John Major, squeezed the centre ground away from the space that had been occupied by the SDP and the Liberals.

The UK Independence Party (UKIP) was formed in 1991. Though it has not done particularly well in Parliamentary elections, only garnering the odd MP, it has had considerable success in European and local elections. Even though it now looks like it is in a state of terminal decline, it too has changed British politics and possibly British history in its key role in the Brexit vote, including possibly the Conservative Party's decision to hold a referendum in the first place so as not to lose votes to UKIP, and the subsequent influence of its former leader, Nigel Farage, on the government's position on Brexit.

> British political history shows that new parties have had considerable impact on the UK's political system

Momentum is not a political party, but its influence on British politics already has been large indeed, and could be even larger. Its 40,000 members and activists have formed a sort of shock troop for the left wing of the Labour Party, keeping Labour leader Jeremy Corbyn in power, ensuring he and his left-wing programme have support within the party. They have been attempting to take the Labour Party down a more radical socialist path then was previously thought acceptable, possibly even more so than the Labour Party of the 1980s under Michael Foot which spawned the SDP.

There have been others, of course – mostly on the extremes (National Front, British National Party, Socialist Workers Party, Workers Socialist League). The Greens have developed from the Ecology Party, mainly via a breakaway faction from the Liberals in the 1970s.

***

British political history has shown that new political parties have regularly had considerable impact on the UK's political system, from ultimately achieving power (The Labour Party), to being a factor in Brexit (UKIP), to radically altering the policies and philosophies of the main parties (SDP). Labour under Jeremy Corbyn, backed by Momentum, could be described as a new/old party with some of the features of insurgent European parties described in the book.

The recent experiences in Europe demonstrate that no incumbent party has a right to exists forever

3

The European landscape

E ven the most parochial Britishers could not help but notice that fairly momentous events have been happening in the rest of the world. In many countries, the old centre-right/centre-left post war settlement seems to have fallen apart (Table 1).

COUNTRY	NEW OR NON-MAINSTREAM PARTIES	MAINSTREAM PARTIES
FRANCE	Emmanuel Macron of La République En Marche (2016) is President with majority in the National Assembly.	Debout Le France and the Socialist Party did not make the run-off for President
	Modem (2007) in alliance with EM for the 2017 legislative elections	Les Republicains remains the largest behind EM.
	La France Insoumise (2016) - 17 assembly seats.	Parti Socialiste has been hit by splits and resulting pitiful 2017 elections.
	Right-wing populist Marine Le Pen of Rassemblement Nationale 2nd in Presidential elections.	
ITALY	Moviemento 5 Stelle (2009) major party in a coalition government. The junior partner, La Lega was itself founded only in 1991.	Italy's tumultuous politics appears to prevent parties growing old and becoming 'traditional'.
	Forza Italia (Berlusconi's party) 106 Deputies and 58 Senators and Partito Democratico (centre-left) - similar	

SPAIN	Unidos Podemos (2016) close second and Ciudadanos (2006) came close 4th	Partido Popular (centre right) held the government until recently.
	Vox (2013 - extreme right) considerable share in 2018 Andalucian election	Partido Socialista Obrero Espanol (centre-left) currently leads minority government
NETHERLANDS	The Party for Freedom (2006)- Right-wing populist has 29 seats in total in both chambers. Modern parties such as 50PLUS, Denk and Forum for democracy all have under 5 seats.	The People's Party for Freedom and Democracy is in government Christian Democratic Appeal, Democrats 66 and Christian Union all have cabinet appointments.
GREECE	Syriza (2012) is largest party and leads government. The River (2014) is centrist, with 6 deputies, whilst the Independent Greeks (2012) have 7 deputies. Golden Dawn (1985) – far-right has 15 deputies.	Panhellenic Socialist Movement (1974) and New Democracy (1974) have 78 and 20 national deputies respectively.
GERMANY	Alternative for Germany (2013- far-right) have 92 deputies The Left (2007) has 69 deputies. Alliance 90/The Greens (1993) have 67 deputies.	The Christian Democratic Union of Germany (1945) and Social Democratic Party (1863) are still the major political parties.
SWEDEN	Sweden Democrats (1988) right wing populist, came 3rd in 2018 elections.	Social Democratic Workers' Party (1889) has 100 seats, the largest. Moderate Party (1904) with 70 seats
POLAND	Law and Justice Party (2001) – right wing populist is now in government with 218 deputies in the Sejm and 59 in Senate.	Few popular parties can claim to be mainstream

	Civic Platform (centrist, 2001) has been in government before - but now has 166 seats altogether.	
HUNGARY	Fidesz (1980s) is a populist illiberal democracy party in government.	Hungarian Socialist Party (1989) and the Christian Democratic People's Party have 16 seats each.
AUSTRIA	Freedom Party (1956), right wing populist party, is junior partner in government.	The Austrian People's Party (centre right) is senior partner in government The Social Democratic Party (centre left) is the second largest party
USA	Populist Bernie Sanders came 2nd in democratic Party nominations and populist reality TV star Donald Trump is President.	The Democratic Party and the Republican Party are to differing extents being taken over by outsiders.

The Fertile Crescent (for new parties)

A full analysis of the social and economic changes that have created the conditions for new parties' recent success is beyond the scope of this book. But there are a few clear common factors.

The political settlement in European countries dates from after the Second World War[1], and the political parties that emerged represented a coalition of interests of the time. For example the Labour Party represented the industrial workers and union movement, socialist intellectuals and returning service men. Since then, these groupings have changed. Though the political parties have tried to change with them they have retained the DNA of the original grouping (for

[1] Or the fall of communism in Central and Eastern Europe, or the end of Iberian dictatorships.

example the influence of trade unions within the Labour Party).

A number of social and economic trends have radically changed the make-up of society, these trends are long-term but have become manifest in recent years. These include: ageing populations, large scale migration, de-industrialisation, globalisation, a move of economies away from manufacturing to services, increase in contract working and decline in employed work.

Many countries in Europe have suffered for many years from high unemployment, in particular amongst the young, and a decrease in job opportunities for less qualified people. This period has seen the rise of women working on approximately equal terms to men, undermining the male breadwinner family model, and the emergence of minority interest groups based on factors such as sexuality and race. There has been a decline in religious observance of the traditional majority or "national" religion alongside the rise of other religions, often from immigrant groups.

> **Broad interest groups in the voting population have radically changed and are no longer reflected in the coalitions of traditional parties**

The result is that the broad interest groups that make up the voting population has radically changed and does not reflect the coalitions represented by traditional parties. For example Corrado Poli describes the rise of the 'profleteriat' in Italy[2], highly educated people doing relatively low paid work, who form the basis of the support of the Five Star Movement.

The way we consume media has also changed: no longer is there a limited choice of trusted TV channels and newspapers.

[2] See Annex

These still exist and are important, but many now consume uncurated news from social media and other sources. At the same time, we have seen the rise of celebrity culture and 24-hour news, and there has been a massive increase in ease of access to information – both true and false. And the corresponding rise in big data means that access (not always legal) to detailed information about people's preferences is available to organisations that can make use of it.

There has been a decline in active political participation (see Figure 1)[3].

Trends in party membership in Europe
Low membership countries, 1960-2010

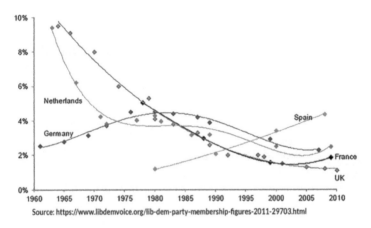

Source: https://www.libdemvoice.org/lib-dem-party-membership-figures-2011-29703.html

This and the decline in social participation have corresponded with a rise of other forms of entertainment with increased pressures on people's time.

[3] Since 2010, there has been an upswing in party membership. Figure 1 shows that all countries except the UK membership was on the rise again. There has been an upswing in the UK as well, where party membership levels have increased back to early 1990s levels, almost entirely due to a large increase in the membership of the Labour Party (House of Commons Briefing Paper Number SN05125 3 September 2018 https://researchbriefings.parliament.uk/ResearchBriefing/Summary/SN05125)

There has been the rise of an expert class as society becomes increasingly complex making it harder for the average voter to understand complex decisions. People therefore have to trust others to take decisions which they may not fully understand on their behalf. This corresponds with less interest in matters discussed by politicians. And politics itself has become another form of entertainment.

> What may be surprising is that new political forces have not emerged sooner

Recent history has also seen the rise in the ideology of the market which encompasses the belief that people get their just rewards for working and that government should stay out of the way of the market, except to ensure the market works well.

The 2008 financial crisis and subsequent Euro crisis had a number of effects. The highly paid financial elite were bailed out by governments, who then imposed austerity on the rest of the population. For many reasons, this was a fatal erosion of the social contract; if people who are highly paid are patently not worth what they are paid, and the government bails them out, this confirms suspicions that there is an elite controlling the economy for their own benefit. The financial crisis showed this elite to be incompetent.

> The financial crisis crystalised tensions and resentments that had been under the surface for a while

The crisis crystalised underlying tensions and resentments that had been under the surface for a while, for example rising inequality, the backlash against immigration, and the drift in the power balance away from workers towards company executives and shareholders.

Since the War, the political spectrum in most Western European countries has included a centre-right party, a centre-left party, each often in coalition with a smaller centre party. Together these parties have dominated the vote. There have been other parties, for example far right and left, green parties and nationalist movements but they have always remained in the fringes.

In all countries, we are seeing the collapse of this centrist dominance, growth of the previous fringe parties, and sometimes the re-invention of the centrist consensus in some other guise.

With this background, it is unsurprising that new political forces have emerged. It is probably more surprising that this did not occur sooner.

4

A process not a party

The political upset, disillusionment and disruption of the decade emerged in response to recession and austerity after the 2008 financial and Euro area crisis. Many economies took a hit, unemployment rose, and disenchantment with politics soon followed.

The four parties that we have studied in detail – *Podemos*, Five Star, *La République En Marche* and the Liberal Party of Canada – along with many other parties all emerged, or re-emerged, in the context of this crisis. But they are not simply reactionary.

> The crisis has led to more support for extreme ideologies and a rewriting of the political rulebook

The emphasis is on 'democracy' – a renewed engagement with governance that promises to focus on public need, as opposed to corporatism or vested interests. These terms, nevertheless, have contested interpretations. These new parties harness technology to reach more people, marketing to them, as well as enabling enhanced engagement. The crisis has led to further support for entrenched and extreme ideologies, but it has also allowed the rewriting of the political rulebook.

Successful new or new/old parties have managed to embody the spirit of insurgency and a challenge to the status quo. Specifically, they have the following in common:

- Parties all have a charismatic leader who portrays him/herself, and is seen, as an outsider

- Critical mass: the party, movement or leader has a critical mass of followers who can form the basis of the party membership

- Coalition of voters: under-represented groups often identify with the parties, especially people who don't usually vote

- Mobilisation: supporters have been mobilised through varied but unconventional use of modern and traditional media

- Recruitment: the parties have attracted supporters from other parties and people new to politics

- Use of data: parties collect and analyse data to tailor image and accurately target voters

- Physical meet-ups: social media facilitates effective physical meetings, which are a key ingredient to success.

- Background conditions: establishment parties appear tired, ineffective, out of touch, compromised, corrupt and/or unrepresentative

- Successful messaging: the parties have all managed to develop and disseminate a successful message along the lines that things are not right, we are different, we/you can change things

Success does not come from the use of social media but from the way that social media are used

It is often thought that the success of the new and new/old parties is because of social media. It is true, that they have all made extensive use of technology, but so have traditional parties with much less success. It is the way they have used it is their determining feature.

A process, not a party

A new party derives its energy and purpose from the process of creating itself, not governing or active politics. Everyone is now trying to use social media, but the successful new parties have used it to mobilise their supporters, and to disseminate an image for the party, embodied in their leader. Social media is used to create, tailor and disseminate this image. This became evident with the one new/old party that we studied, the Canadian Liberal Party. But understanding *how* they deployed technology is the key to interpreting the success of the genuinely new parties.

> Successful insurgent parties have used a similar process that works irrespective of the parties' policies or ideologies

The structure of new parties can be thought of as a process rather than a traditional hierarchical party. The process works irrespective of the party's policies or ideological origins.

The adjacent figure characterises the structure of a traditional political party. It is typically hierarchical, with decisions taken at the top, but then honed, shaped and implemented by the various levels of the party machinery.

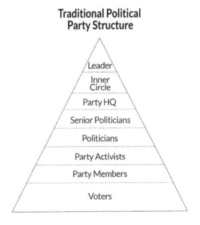

Traditional Political Party Structure

Leader
Inner Circle
Party HQ
Senior Politicians
Politicians
Party Activists
Party Members
Voters

In contrast, new parties have a different organisational philosophy (see figure). The leader and his inner circle have direct contact with the party's followers. Compared to a traditional party, there is less demarcation between followers. Communication is directed by a facilitator, who is in charge of the channels of communication and the data gathering.

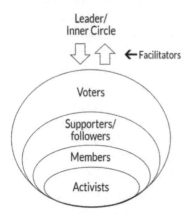

New Party Structure

Leader/
Inner Circle

← Facilitators

Voters

Supporters/
followers

Members

Activists

In contrast to a traditional party, the new party lacks a hierarchy of politicians, which is ultimately a key weakness, to be discussed later in the book.

If we were to look further into the organisation of the new party, we would not find an amorphous mass of followers but something more like a social or political network of connected people, with some followers acting like hubs, with multiple connections.

Four stages of development

We have identified four stages of the new party process. First, the new party needs to recruit a critical mass of followers. The second stage is that lines of constant, two-way communication are established between the leader and the followers to establish a bond, mobilise the followers, and create a conversation or stream of information from the followers that the party can use.

> The new political party is a social network of connections. Some followers act as hubs with multiple connections.

The third stage is the mobilisation of followers using social media and technology to organise meaningful physical interactions between followers and between followers and the public. These interactions occur on a regular basis – not just around election time. They have the triple purpose of converting supporters into activists, collecting data and information from the meetings and facilitating interaction between activists and the wider public.

The last stage, and possibly the key function of this interaction and data gathering, is for the party and leader to create and tailor their image and accurately disseminate their message. This is achieved using the already established communication channels.

A characteristic to emphasise is the self-organising nature of these movements. Most political parties want to maintain central control over everything that goes on. The three new parties studied encourage their followers to self-organise locally.

> Image and process cannot be dissociated. The appeal lies in the self-organising, democratic nature with followers actively influencing policy

The image and the process cannot be dissociated – the image and the appeal of the parties is that they are self-organising and democratic, with followers determining the policies.

We describe each of the stages here.

Stage 1: Recruitment

The process needs a critical mass of followers. Five Stars, for example, grew from an initial pool of Beppe Grillo's fans to a large organisation through the readership of Grillo's online blog (which became one of the most widely read blogs in Europe). In the case of the Canadian Liberal Party these were existing party members. *Podemos* grew out of an anti-austerity protest – the 15-m Movement.

The first use of social media is to facilitate communication lines between and among the followers and with the leader, but directed by a facilitator, who controls the 'software' of the party.

Stage 2: Constant communication – creating activists

There is a big difference between having followers who like your tweets, party members who leaflet in the run up to elections, and the self-directed, enthused or even angry supporters of movements such as Five Stars – who actively organise meetings and formulate policy. The key is a constant two-way conversation between party and supporters.

> There is a big difference between followers liking your tweets and distributing leaflets, and the self-directed, enthused and angry supporters of these new movements

Parties' websites and social media accounts comment on current political goings-on in real time. Five Stars uses this to a great degree – elected politicians, including the party's Deputy Prime Minister Luigi Di Maio, publicly comment on political debates and criticise other figures of Italian society on an official blog.[4]

Podemos's main membership was built up through *La Tuerka*, a show created by Pablo Iglesias and his fellow activists and run on a local Madrid television channel since 2010. It was from the popularity of this show – watched across Spain via video-sharing websites – that *Podemos* founders

[4] https://www.buzzfeednews.com/article/albertonardelli/luigi-di-maio-matteo-salvini-donald-trump

knew a real party had the potential to work. *La Tuerka* is a debate show – it aims to persuade viewers by entertaining them; for example Iglesias fronts a show called *Fort Apache*, broadcast to South America via an Iranian state channel, in which he rides a motorcycle and whoops like John Wayne.[5] Five Stars mirrors this in Beppe Grillo's politically-driven comedy and Casaleggio Associati's network of tabloid-like blogs and news sites.[6]

In the most popular channels of communication, parties speak directly to their fanbase. The intentionally non-mainstream bent of *La Tuerka*, the entertaining blog posts of Beppe Grillo, keep people engaged whilst underlining the parties' anti-establishment convictions. Five Stars only relatively recently collaborated with mainstream newspapers and television channels – their distaste for the political status quo previously prevented them from talking to outlets they considered media elites.[7]

Macron has none of Five Stars' anger, but he, too, appreciated the use of direct online communication. Looking friendly with traditional outlets is not the required image. Five Stars and *Podemos* gathered supporters through direct channels. Interviews with journalists and articles in magazines only target those who are not necessarily the most responsive to online marketing or adverts.[8]

[5]https://www.theguardian.com/world/2015/mar/31/podemos-revolution-radical-academics-changed-european-politics

[6] https://www.buzzfeed.com/albertonardelli/italys-most-popular-political-party-is-leading-europe-in-fak

[7] https://radix.org.uk/five-stars-dreaming-radically-new-politics/

[8] From interviews.

Stage 3: Mobilisation of followers – data gathering and physical meetings

New parties are built in today's technologically-minded world but have realised the importance of old-fashioned non-virtual interaction. Interested persons can find local En Marche committees through dedicated pages on its website.[9] Re-energised door-knocking efforts from the Liberal Party of Canada and En Marche have been more than complemented by connections made with the public via social media sites. In the case of the Canadian Liberals, people were e-invited to rallies on Twitter, Facebook and email, and then signed-up as on-the-ground door-knockers.[10]

> Connections with the public through social media have complemented and re-energised door-knocking efforts

Five Stars' *Rousseau* internet platform signs up members and gives them a space to shape party policy via debate forums and online polls. The membership has unprecedented control, holding primaries for EU parliamentary candidates on party lists (unknown in Italy) and thereafter rendering elected officials as conduits for their will. Polls were taken before votes, binding Five Stars deputies.[11] *Podemos*, though less innovative, uses

[9] From interviews

[10] https://ipolitics.ca/2018/03/21/team-trudeau-and-the-liberals-facebook-conundrum/

[11] https://www.ft.com/content/546be098-989f-11e7-a652-cde3f882dd7b; https://www.opendemocracy.net/can-europe-make-it/lorenzo-del-savio-matteo-mameli/antirepresentative-democracy-how-to-understand-fi

similar online debate tools, and is creating a new app for instant mass polling.[12]

In comparison, *En Marche* and the Canadian Liberal Party have less insurgent visions of e-democracy, but it is a mistake to categorise them as old-fashioned. Emmanuel Macron set out on a *Grande Marche*, alongside volunteers, in the year before elections.[13]

From 25,000 surveys with people on doorsteps, Macron "diagnosed" the country's ills, and subsequently laid out his political platform. Macron has guiding principles, but it is notable that he took care to show he listened to a wide array of people (at least before he came to power).[14] Technology can encourage a pragmatic or technocratic approach

> A leader who listens, and is seen to be listening, is key to capturing the public mood and energising a supporter base

to politics. Though the Liberal Party does not come close to the others' futurism in organising its infrastructure, it has made considerable efforts to expand its rank-and-file. From an almost non-existent volunteer base, it grew to 80,000 activists during the 2015 election.[15] The party has expanded, even though members do not develop policy Five Stars-style.

The flipside to listening to voters' concerns is gathering voters' data. Information gathering and processing has become easier with technology and available to most well-

[12]https://www.theguardian.com/world/2015/mar/31/podemos-revolution-radical-academics-changed-european-politics;

[13] From interviews

[14]https://venturebeat.com/2017/01/08/meet-the-french-presidential-candidate-whos-using-the-internet-to-reinvent-politics/

[15] https://www.youtube.com/watch?v=tbRWkz4zLtE

funded organisations, even, presumably, in the post-Cambridge Analytica age. *En Marche* commissioned an app to allow volunteers to collect opinions on the doorstep; the Liberal Party had *The Console* of voters and constituencies ranked in win-ability.[16]

Stage 4: Use of data: create image and disseminate messages

A key function of creating activists is to feedback information to tailor the message and image of the party.

> Communication with the voter base is two-way and virtually uninterrupted 24/7. Campaigning never stops

Communication is virtually uninterrupted. The public can be persuaded, online, at any time. The 24/7 access of the internet means campaigning never really stops.[17]

In the case of Five Stars, the image and message are that the party is democratic, open source and anti-establishment. Five Stars' policies have been created by their followers – this is a key selling point because this is their appeal, rather than for the importance of the policies themselves.

The Canadian Liberals found that people liked Trudeau's youth, freshness, and "sunny ways". They also wanted a change and something different from the establishment, all of which Trudeau had in abundance. But, from information gathered, it was found that they needed to be reassured – this was used to tailor his message towards relatability and

[16] From interviews and https://ipolitics.ca/2018/03/21/team-trudeau-and-the-liberals-facebook-conundrum/

[17] https://www.thestar.com/news/insight/2015/06/05/the-permanent-campaign-is-now-a-canadian-institution-delacourt.html

authenticity. Trudeau uses frequent communication via social media to project this image: Facebook is for friends – Trudeau takes part in the platform's "60-Second Challenge", answering rapid-fire questions about his personal life. Knowing his favourite food or how many times his children have watched *Frozen* is not obviously correlated with how good a Prime Minister he would be. But it is part of building an image of "relatability and authenticity".[18]

Podemos tries to capture the public mood and uses it to present a pathway. It is left-wing and offers left-wing policies - but understanding that this might alienate much of the population, these policies are always framed as a reasoned and balanced response to contemporary problems.

> The ability constantly to tailor the message according to voter feedback is possibly the main function – and the main success factor – of the mobilisation and activism of the movement

Podemos adapts to modern politics without losing some conventional strengths: the membership exercises its voice through membership "circles", but internal structures mean *Podemos* is still an electoral party rather than a social movement. *Podemos* has an in-depth understanding of modern Spanish media. It has built a support base on one TV channel, whilst avoiding alienating the rest of the population on other channels.

Podemos is a party that knows its audience.

---

[18] http://policymagazine.ca/pdf/16/PolicyMagazineNovemberDecember-2015-Chan.pdf

The ability to tailor the message is possibly the main function of the mobilisation and activism of the movement. As the message is honed, it then needs to be disseminated.

Using the data gathered, voters are targeted. Macron used surveys to adapt his speeches to the concerns of regions he was speaking in.[19] French law allows televised campaigns only during the last two weeks of a campaign. *En Marche* could target adverts at that time towards older generations who still respond to this channel of communication. But younger people (at this time, 50 years and below) were reached for some months before that with targeted clips on social media.[20]

Technology creates problems of its own and divided communication can further divide a populace. In the online networks created by *Podemos* and *En Marche*, supporters talk to others with similar principles and viewpoints. This can be positive. *Podemos* has an online group for differently-abled people, where physical impediments or geographic isolation might otherwise not allow for this.[21]

On the other hand, the creation of echo-chambers is inevitable. Five Stars, cutting-edge on many fronts, has taken this to an extreme. The organisation, through *Casaleggio Associati*, has built an entire network of websites and social media accounts, which, for many supporters, function as the majority of their media intake.[22]

Direct communication between party leadership and voters can seem like engagement, but it can also erode balanced

---

[19] From interviews

[20] From interviews

[21]https://www.theguardian.com/world/2015/mar/31/podemos-revolution-radical-academics-changed-european-politics

[22] https://www.ft.com/content/546be098-989f-11e7-a652-cde3f882dd7b

assessment. The breakdown in local communities which Corrado Poli has observed in his native Italy, is part-and-parcel of this untethered cloud of curated opinion. The new, streamlined media has done away with conventional checks on the aggregation of influence.

This is not specific to the European context – recently-elected Brazilian President Bolsonaro has been bolstered by an "army" who use popular messaging service WhatsApp to circulate fake news and censor dissenting opinion.[23]

[23] https://www.theguardian.com/world/2018/oct/25/brazil-president-jair-bolsonaro-whatsapp-fake-news

5

Characteristics and shortcomings

The Outsiders v The Elite

A ll the parties studied display traits associated with populism, most conspicuously *Podemos* and Five Stars. Both parties use the term *la casta*, an example of what Giles Tremlett of *The Guardian* terms *"simple, emotionally engaging rhetoric"*, to refer to the domestic and EU establishment.[24] The sense here is very much a *"we the people"*, against *"the elites"*, the politicians and their funders who have dominated power for many years.

En Marche and the Liberal Party of Canada are far less combative, yet they, too, register this trend. Emmanuel Macron held his candidacy announcement in a community meeting of his hometown of Amiens underlining a connection to his roots, given that French presidential candidates usually hold a press conference separated from ordinary voters.[25] The Liberal Party is anomalous amongst the surveyed as being a long-established party. Yet Justin Trudeau casts himself as an outsider on behalf of the people against the Conservative government status-quo; supporting the squeezed middle-class and pledging to increase government spending.

[24]https://www.theguardian.com/world/2015/mar/31/podemos-revolution-radical-academics-changed-european-politics;
http://blogs.lse.ac.uk/europpblog/2018/05/24/the-five-star-movement-and-the-rise-of-techno-populist-parties/

[25] From interviews

This messaging carries weight with a disenfranchised public: the system is run by the elites for the elites. The people no longer count and are not listened to. Macron deliberately distanced himself from his former *Parti Socialiste*, with this in mind.

> Message: The system is run by the elites for the elites. You are not listened to and no longer count.

Turnout figures have suggested that the Liberals' campaign attracted abstainers and other non-voters.[26] Winning isn't about convincing existing voter to switch parties but people who would not otherwise vote. The likes of Five Stars and *Podemos* address the wishes of a pool of people willing to vote for a new alternative.

All parties had a response to the financial crisis and subsequent austerity. In the case of the four surveyed, it was predominantly to be radically different from the government in power and attempting to take away the pain from ordinary people.

Don Butler of *The Ottawa Citizen* suggested that the Liberal Party's deficit promises made them distinct from their competitors.[27] The other two Canadian parties fought over who could best deliver similar messages, whilst the Liberals stood out. Back in Europe, Five Stars delivered a radical response – it eschews traditional ideology in favour of pragmatism, arguing for practical solutions to contemporary problems.[28] Macron follows a similar line, presenting what

[26] https://ottawacitizen.com/news/politics/how-justin-trudeau-liberals-really-won

[27] https://ottawacitizen.com/news/politics/how-justin-trudeau-liberals-really-won

[28]http://blogs.lse.ac.uk/europpblog/2018/05/24/the-five-star-movement-and-the-rise-of-techno-populist-parties/

policies he had as thoughtful and educated counters to issues the public has identified

The rejection of ideology is a key part of the messaging of these new parties. Old parties have ideologies – this has failed, the new parties are therefore different as they reject the notion of having an ideology at all – they have practical, common sense solutions, even policies developed by the voters themselves. At least this is their messaging.

> The rejection of ideology in favour of pragmatism – practical solutions to contemporary problems – is a key feature of new movements

In contrast to his election opponents, Macron, for example, promised no overarching political ideologies or allegiances (although it could be argued that, now in power, he is governing along standard neo-liberal ideological lines). Even Marine Le Pen, presidential candidate for the right-wing *Front National* (now the *Rassemblement National* – National Rally) may have looked the more stereotypical populist, but Macron's own approach was in tune with the public sentiment.

In a world where the establishment is no longer valued, traditions carry less weight with the modern voting public, *En Marche* and Five Stars profess to share a distaste for professional politics – the latter wishes to limit the terms of those serving in parliament to two terms, whilst *En Marche* set aside candidacies for people who had never sought office before.[29]

Macron, formerly of the *Parti Socialiste*, dropped all associations with the historic, left of centre party. The first *En Marche* website was completely white – absent of colours that

[29] From interviews

have variously associated with socialism, conservatism, ecoism and others.[30]

Podemos, meanwhile, is most certainly left-wing in its policies. But in marketing itself, it refrains from delving back into the old tribal discussions of Spain's past. Pablo Iglesias, *Podemos's* General Secretary, has said reference to old symbols hurts his party. The old armies look tired and out-of-place in this modern world. When Iglesias was invited onto conservative-leaning, televised talk-shows, he presents *Podemos's* political platform as common sense.[31] *Podemos's* founders are categorically left-wing, but they know how to play to their audience.

> The leader has become the defining feature of the new movements

The Leader as substitute for ideology

One apparent contradiction of this democratic wave is that all four parties have dominating charismatic leaders.

En Marche was set-up specifically to elect its founder, Emmanuel Macron, whose initials it duplicates. The first activists of Five Stars were followers of the comedian Beppe Grillo. Trudeau and Iglesias are practically synonymous with the parties they lead. Corrado Poli, an academic expert on Five Stars, suggests that, because the parties eschew ideologies, the party is embodied by the leader.[32]

[30] From interviews

[31] https://newleftreview.org/II/93/pablo-iglesias-understanding-podemos

[32] https://radix.org.uk/five-stars-dreaming-radically-new-politics/

Certainly in the cases of *En Marche* and the Liberal Party, leaders make the final calls.[33] Even *Podemos*, which grew through autonomous circles of local grassroots activists, quickly recognised centralised power eight months after it was founded: their – its member-created EU campaign manifesto was "impractical and uncosted" and included such promises as the *"non-payment of illegitimate debt"*.[34]

The leader has become the defining feature of the party. For Five Stars, *En Marche* and *Podemos*, party machinery has been created, but mainly to make the organisation function, running its online forums and managing campaign material.

The political alliances of older parties, be it civil organisations like Countryside Alliances or trade unions, are not there. Members, and by extension, voters, are listened to directly.

Perhaps a strong leader means a strong advocate in government, but leaders become the main draw: Pablo Iglesias, one of *Podemos's* founders, made such a name for himself through the media that his face became the party's logo for the 2014 EU elections, after a poll showed 42 per cent more people recognised him than his party.[35]

Leaders' guidance can also invigorate, as is clear with Justin Trudeau, head of the Canadian Liberals. Inexperienced and under pressure to begin with, he both made momentous alterations to party organisation and programme and

[33] https://ottawacitizen.com/news/politics/how-justin-trudeau-liberals-really-won; https://www.newstatesman.com/culture/2017/06/new-french-revolution-how-en-marche-disrupted-politics

[34]https://www.theguardian.com/world/2015/mar/31/podemos-revolution-radical-academics-changed-european-politics; https://newleftreview.org/II/93/pablo-iglesias-understanding-podemos

[35]https://www.theguardian.com/world/2015/mar/31/podemos-revolution-radical-academics-changed-european-politics

meaningfully connected to voters.[36] The specific leaders' characteristics might not sell in the UK – Grillo, although charismatic, is also vulgar, whilst Macron mentions more philosophy in his speeches than any British politician would know, let alone publicly admit that they did. Nonetheless, finding the right candidate will be essential to the success of any potential party in the UK.

An extreme version of leader-as-party can often be found in the right-wing new parties. In the Netherlands, Geert Wilders, the Leader of the Party of Freedom, for a long time **was** the Party of Freedom – being its only member. In Italy, Five Stars' coalition partner is *La Lega*, led by Matteo Salvini, who is very much synonymous with the party.

It is true that traditional mainstream parties can often be dominated by one leader: think Margaret Thatcher, Tony Blair or Angela Merkel. But compared to the new parties, these old parties have other centres of power to temper the leader's power.

Flaws in the Machine

The process which has brought about spectacular election success for new parties contains the flaws that may lead to their ultimate decline. They manifest themselves once they achieve political power. As a new party derives its energy and purpose from the process of creating itself, not from governing or being a serious political force, once it attains power it faces a crisis.

Then again, these new movements are not unique in facing existential decline once they enter government. As the Liberal Democrats in the UK, the Labour Party in the Netherlands, the FDP and the SDP in Germany, and others have shown, entering government, often in coalition with others, can be

[36] http://site.macleans.ca/longform/trudeau/index.html

fatal or near fatal even for long-established, traditional parties. Conversely, *La Lega* in Italy has soared in popularity once it took the reins of government and Matteo Salvini, its highly effective and charismatic leader, used the platform of Deputy Prime Minister to overshadow the Five Stars Movement.

Concentration of power

The problems tend to boil down to too much concentration of power (either in the leader and his inner circle, or with the controller of the party's platform), opacity of decision-making process, lack of expert oversight of party's policies, and an inability to incorporate dissenting views.

Parties are often not prepared for actual participation in the political process once the party gets into power. They are not able to translate the energy of building a party full of hope into actual governing or participation in the political process. *La Lega* may be the exception that proves the rule. Or it may be that Salvini is, so far, the only leader who has shown himself able, when in government, to keep driving the same energy that yielded electoral success.

> New movements derive their energy and purpose from the process of creating themselves, not from governing or being a 'serious' political force

At first glance, the problems of *En Marche* and the Canadian Liberals compared to Five Stars should be very different. The analysis in this paper, in line with many media critiques, portrays *En Marche* and the Canadian Liberals as being run by a small coterie of the leader plus his trusted advisors, with clever use of technology to appear close to the people. In contrast, Five Stars is seen as being too democratic, with policies developed by supporters which are inconsistent and often unrealistic. In fact, the flaws have the same ultimate causes.

If we take the case of Five Stars; it has been accused of both being too supporter-driven and too elite. In early parliamentary years, the party expelled deputies who did not follow the outcome of an "official" online poll. Deputies were not meant to have a free mandate – the very concept of a representative democratic system was challenged by this new political organisation.[37]

Almost paradoxically, the entire party was built around a single man, Beppe Grillo, supported by a private business called *Casaleggio Associati*, now run by Davide Casaleggio, which fulfils the facilitator function (described in the figure on page 28). The streamlined structure of the party leaves no checks on power, and *"no formal mechanisms for party members to challenge Mr Casaleggio's leadership"*.[38] The supporters whose deputies so doggedly serve cannot guarantee their leadership's loyalty. What's more, *Casaleggio Associati* controls the media sites that are the focal point for Five Stars supporters and their views.

It remains to be seen whether this will change now that Five Stars are in power, led by Luigi Di Maio as deputy Prime Minister. Grillo was never seen as a future leader of the country as he was always clear that he would not run for office. And Di Maio does not have the same public appeal as did Grillo.

Further down the scale, old problems of traditional parties still exist. Membership of *Podemos*, for instance, has become staggered in levels of members' involvement. Leader Iglesias

[37]https://www.opendemocracy.net/can-europe-make-it/lorenzo-del-savio-matteo-mameli/antirepresentative-democracy-how-to-understand-fi

[38] https://www.ft.com/content/546be098-989f-11e7-a652-cde3f882dd7b

has reached heights of celebrity-like status. This might explain why Iglesias won his leadership bid within the organisation, though many who had supported *Podemos* from the beginning wanted a three-person executive to mitigate centralised power.[39]

Hierarchies of participation persist. *Podemos, En Marche* and Five Stars all have intentionally easy sign-up systems, there is no assurance of in-depth checks on members' identity or background. Subsequent online polls come with no assurances that people are well-informed. Turnouts may be dominated by certain radical sections of activists, skewing the result.

Ultimately though, the organisational structures depicted in the figures above imply the source of new party's shortcomings. The new party process is lacking a middle tier of career politicians. These normally provide expertise in formulating practical policies and checks and balances between the leader and party membership.

> Open source policies may not get the benefit of experience to hone good ideas into coherent policy platforms

In a traditional party, the leader and his or her policy team, have policies overseen and amended by the senior party politicians (in the UK context this would be the Cabinet or Shadow Cabinet), who also have to be mindful that policies have to be agreed upon by politicians. New parties lack these checks and balances. In the case of leader-dominated parties; the leader formulates policies without any sense checks. In the case of *uber*-democratic parties, the open source policies do

[39]https://www.theguardian.com/world/2015/mar/31/podemos-revolution-radical-academics-changed-european-politics

not get the benefit of experienced politicians honing what may be good ideas into coherent policies.

New parties also have trouble incorporating dissenting views. *Podemos* and Five Stars control their own news dissemination channels, which inevitably will lead to echo chamber effects. Parties run by an inner circle can end up out of touch and subject to group think. The case of Five Stars shows that democracy itself can stifle debate.

It remains to be seen whether, once in power these parties develop experienced cadres.

It must be said that in response to the 2008 crisis, all four parties we have examined have sought to embody a sense of positive change and hope. With corruption scandals amongst Spain's established parties, to the unpalatable historic associations of France's *Front National*, it is little wonder politicians were considered out-of-touch and reproachable.

> In response to the 2008 crisis, all insurgent parties have embodied a sense of positive change and hope

Renewed connection with the public has thus been at the heart of many new political movements. *Podemos's* name translates as "we can", which exemplifies this belief. Five Stars serves in the Italian coalition known as the "Government of Change". The past can be recognised and the future envisioned, as Trudeau did in his "sunny ways" story articulated during the election campaign and into government.[40] Macron appealed to underlying values and reminded voters that some principles should not be discarded lightly.

It remains to be seen whether these new parties are ephemeral phenomena. Now that they are in power, can they

---

[40] https://www.liberal.ca/the-sunny-way/

persist as a process, not a party? Or will they turn themselves into more traditional parties? Or will the new parties disappear as quickly as they emerged, and if so, what will replace them – will a second wave of new parties arise, as the pathway to power has been established by the first wave, or will the traditional parties return, maybe adopting some of the techniques of the new parties?

6

Cracking the UK

All of the factors that gave rise to new parties in Europe and other countries exist in abundance in Britain. The UK is no different in this respect to other European countries. The UK's political landscape has been dominated by centre-right and centre-left parties. The UK has experienced the same social and economic trends since the war as other European countries, and indeed the impact of the financial crisis and the resultant austerity were especially pronounced, as the UK is particularly dependent on financial services.

> All the factors that gave rise to new parties in Europe exist in abundance in the UK

Though Labour and the Conservatives pre-date the Second World War, and have local differences to equivalent European parties, they are built on similar coalitions of interests which, today, no longer reflect the make-up of the population. Before the emergence of Jeremy Corbyn, membership of political parties had fallen even more rapidly in the UK than in other countries. Following the financial crisis, and with the shambles of Brexit and the internal fighting in the Labour party, the perceived competence of the traditional political parties is at an all-time low – and Labour Party membership is falling again.

It could be argued that a new/old party has already emerged, in the left-wing organisation Momentum, which has been crucial to the rise and support of Jeremy Corbyn as the leader of the Labour party. Momentum is estimated to have 40,000 members and crucially a high proportion are activists.[41] Momentum also employs many of the new party tactics described in this book.

What will it take?

Drawing on the lessons from other countries, it is fairly straightforward to outline the factors required for a new political party.

First, a highly effective leader is required. He or she will probably, but not necessarily, come from outside politics. They need to be popular and charismatic with the ability to inspire and enthuse people.

> An effective leader needs to be more 'celebrity' than 'traditional politician'

They need to be able to portray themselves as outside the establishment. They need to be to some extent anti-political, in that they are willing to say the unsayable without being damaged. This does not mean they have to be Donald Trump-style offensive, but that they are not constrained by typical political or party narratives and inherent conservatism and risk aversion.

The leader has to have more of the characteristics of a celebrity than of a traditional member of the political class.

Another factor is a large, critical mass, of social media followers. This could be followers of the leader him/herself, or it could arise from a movement, gathering or protest.

The media platform is crucial to the success of a party, but it is also not really a barrier. A number of platforms have been successfully developed, for example *Rousseau* used by the Five Stars movement. *Podemos* and Five Stars provide far wider communication channels than just social media, involving

[41] https://www.independent.co.uk/news/uk/politics/momentum-membership-jeremy-corbyn-green-party-40000-labour-nec-jon-lansman-a8286706.html

news outlets and TV channels. This may or may not be possible in the UK, given that the UK is fairly dominated by mainstream media. On the other hand, there may be opportunities, as the potential target voter for a new party may not feel well served by the current media choice.

The First Past the Post System

An obvious barrier in the UK is the first past the post (FPTP) voting system. The candidate in each voting district with the most number of votes is elected, whereas the other parties standing receive no representation from their votes. Leaving aside whether this is a good system or not, purely mathematically it favours parties with a strong regional focus (for example the Scottish Nationalist Party (SNP)) and dis-favours smaller parties whose vote is relatively evenly spread.

The most egregious example of this was in the 1983 general election when the SDP/Liberal Alliance received 25 per cent of the vote but only won 23 seats[42]. In contrast with the 2015 general election where the SNP won 56 seats with 4.7 per cent of the national vote (although 50% in Scotland)[43]. However, even in a national vote there seems to be a threshold over which there is a non-linear relationship between votes and seats.

The figure on the next page shows the relationship between votes and seats in all UK general elections since 1945 for all parties.

It shows that between 26 and 30 per cent of the vote represents a threshold – if a party can get over this barrier then there will be a large and disproportional increase in the number of seats the receive for their vote. This is also the level

[42]http://news.bbc.co.uk/onthisday/hi/dates/stories/june/9/newsid_2500000/2500847.stm
[43]http://www.electoralcommission.org.uk/__data/assets/pdf_file/0006/190959/UKPGE-report-May-2015-1.pdf

above which a party will come second in an election (as opposed to third).

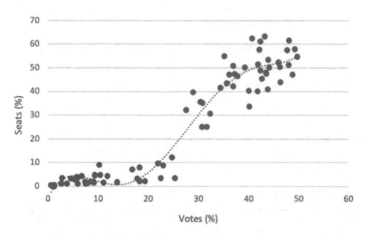

UK parties have significant success if they can crack the 26-30% threshold

The Liberal Party, Alliance or Liberal Democrats have always fallen short, though they have at times come very close, to this level. If a new party could surmount this barrier, FPTP would work in its favour and it would swallow up the votes of the previous second party. In Europe, as described earlier, many new parties have crossed this threshold which means the voter split between the traditional parties has worked in their favour.

Even if it could be possible for a new party to break the 26-30 per cent threshold, FTPT is such an obvious barrier that it has proved a discouragement to new parties. Yet we do not think it is an insurmountable one.

Not all UK elections are FTPT; mayoral elections work on a single transferrable vote system, city assemblies are voted by proportional representation, as are elections to European Parliaments (if these were ever to occur again in the UK).

Given that the FTPT voting system favours regional parties and that some of the non-general election opportunities – for example in mayoral and city assembly elections – could be captured by a party targeted at these localities, one of the design features of the new party could be to have regional appeal. As discussed, the SNP ends up disproportionately represented in parliament. Maybe in the UK local politics is the key to later success in national politics.

In national elections, a party can get beyond the threshold if voters believe it can get beyond the threshold. If they don't believe that, then they will not vote for it because it's a wasted vote. So, one needs to get them to believe.

> In national elections a party can get beyond the threshold if voters believe it can get beyond the threshold

This can be achieved by focusing on creating the network first and showing the widespread support before election time. Success in the non-national elections could also overcome this belief barrier.

The electoral success of many new movements has favoured certain regions – famously Trump's rust belt supporters, or Recap Erdogan's Anatolian heartland. Centrist parties have more trouble, as their support is generally more evenly spread. However, Five Stars conquered the cities first (with variable success when they took them over) and the centrist Citizens Party (*Ciudadanos*) in Spain was originally a Catalonian party.

It is not surprising that Five Stars first won in cities; their biggest appeal is to young urbanists. They started out by focusing on large scale meet-ups in cities – the famous V-Day started in Bologna in 2007.

Britain also has a long traditional of organised protest meetings in cities and it is not beyond imagination that these could be coalesced into political movements. From these movements it is also possible that suitable leaders could emerge who could stand in mayoral elections. With these bases, the new party could dedicate resources to fighting general elections in seats in or near their base.

Other barriers are often cited as why a new party could not get off the ground in the UK. These include a lack of funding, a hostile media, the voter lists of the traditional parties. All of these have existed in other countries and none have been a barrier to the emergence of new parties.

Funding does not seem to be a problem; the process described above generates its own funding, if set up correctly. The new parties have often revelled in a hostile media, as they can then portray themselves as the enemy of the establishment. They have developed their own media sources which provide supporters with alternative sources of news.

> All other factors cited in the UK as barriers to success for a new party exist elsewhere and have not proven to be real blocks to success

Voter lists also have not been an issue, the parties target people who haven't voted. The mobilisation of activists to collect data in effect makes parties' voter lists redundant.

Although many of the people involved in new parties are new to politics, the parties have been successful in recruiting party members from other parties. This is a crucial part of their success as they have the detailed knowledge of the workings of the electoral and political system. These people are generally lower level – they are not the equivalent of MPs but councillors or party activists.

In the UK, there is a strong tribalism amongst traditional parties which acts as a barrier to people switching. But a new party would face these psychological barriers to a much lesser extent. Momentum, albeit not a party as such, has successfully recruited other party activists. It would not be hard to imagine party members at the right wing of the Labour party or

Remainer Conservatives switching if there were a credible alternative.

What is highly unlikely to work is a new party that simply represents a re-badging of the old political class led by some re-cycled politician wanting a second bite at the cherry, with the same habits and churning out the same political language that everyone is tired of.

> **Re-cycling the same old traditional politics is unlikely to work**

A new party may not necessarily have the objective of winning a general election. It could be argued that the SDP and UKIP were both a great success even though they did not win many seats at general elections. The SDP changed British politics for the two decades following its demise and UKIP made a major contribution to the UK's decision to leave the EU.

The process of a new political party could work from any section of the political spectrum, and, as we have already argued, Momentum has effectively created a new/old left party. The insurgent right party, UKIP, is apparently in a state of terminal decline, with which situation the authors of this paper are quite satisfied. There is an obvious gap in the market for a new centre party.

> **The process of a new political party could work from any part of the political spectrum**

There are though, existing centre parties – obviously the Liberal Democrats and the Greens, if the latter could be defined as such. A new party would have to compete with these parties for centrist votes.

The Liberal Democrats have a large and growing membership[44] - at around 100,000, nearly the same as the Conservatives – which could form the required critical mass. They are also looking to recruit a leader by way of an open source vote. If they can pull that off and attract a leader with the right characteristics as described above – and if they can truly transform themselves into something that captures the zeitgeist, a tall order given how wedded most parties are to their traditional, if tired and irrelevant, ways of doing things – they could have the potential to transform themselves into a new/old party like the Canadian Liberals.

> Established parties may be too wedded to their old ways to transform themselves in any meaningful way

If they achieve this, they may crowd out the possibility of a new centrist party. But if they do not, they are faced with the threat of being made irrelevant by the emergence of a new centrist party.

It is also possible, but less likely, that this could be the case with the Greens. The Green Party in Germany has turned itself into a successful mainstream party and the Five Stars movement have many environmental concerns and policies. But the Green Party in the UK is currently too small to take too many votes from a large-scale movement and, because of its size and specialist concerns, it will be immune to the impact of such a movement.

How to correct the flaws in the design

If a new party were to emerge in the UK and achieve electoral success, it should learn lessons from other European countries to avoid their failings once they have achieved success.

[44] https://researchbriefings.parliament.uk/ResearchBriefing/Summary/SN05125

This book has argued that the flaws that manifest themselves when new parties come to power are inherent in the design of the parties. Yet, given that we know what these are, there are also ways and means to avoid them.

First, concentration of power in the leader. Ironically there is a tendency for these highly democratic parties to become authoritarian, the parties themselves being embodied by a charismatic leader. The leader and his inner circle make all of the policy decisions. The charismatic leader is a key element of success.

> Ironically, these highly democratic parties tend to become authoritarian

Once elected, the leader becomes too absorbed with the burdens of governing and gives up talking to people (*cf.* Macron). Yet *La Lega*'s Salvini has shown that this is not inevitable. He has recognised that political life must be a constant electoral campaign and that the business of government cannot be allowed to get in the way of a leader's inexorable campaigning at national level. And even while co-heading the government, Salvini and di Maio have managed to maintain their insurgent, anti-establishment credentials intact – largely by shifting their ire towards the EU as the embodiment of the detached establishment. Not for them Macron's damaging gilded palaces image.

Parties can also be too democratic, with members formulating policies, which then become unrealistic or lack coherence. In these situations, there can be too much concentration of power in the controller of the platform on which the party relies, and a lack of transparency in the process of policy-making via this platform.

Because the structure is as previously described, there is a direct relationship between the leader and his followers, but a lack of expert politicians and policymakers to temper what the leader and his followers want with the practicalities of policy-making. A new party should therefore actively look to recruit these. They need not be actual politicians; they could be political scientists or journalists or experts in other fields. These people need to perform the important function of overseeing policy and the development of the party.

> Traditional parties can have the same flaws as new parties – and without the advantages

Once again, this issue is not limited to the new parties. The disastrous 2017 Conservative Party election campaign was a centralised affair focused on Theresa May – who has absolutely none of the leadership features we describe here. Jeremy Corbyn has taken to making policy with a small inner circle and ignoring the expressed wishes of both his parliamentary party and the wider membership – for example on Brexit policy.

The parties also need other power centres besides the leader. A regional approach might work well; if new party candidates stood in mayoral elections, they would become charismatic alternative figureheads to the leader.

The process of policy-making and engagement are crucial. Five Stars' open source policy-making is in principle a good idea, if tempered with expert opinion to turn the good ideas into a coherent and realistic whole. This democratic process, if adopted by Macron and Trudeau, for example, could temper their seeming out-of-touchness. But the platform

> Open source policy making can work if tempered with expert opinion to create a realistic whole

that delivers the policy also has to be open source or at least transparent, as is the decision-making process of how policies get adopted.

Just like it does not guarantee success, technology alone does not give rise to the problems articulated. These lie in the way technology has been deployed.

Modern technology can provide abundant ways for parties to manage themselves. There is no reason why an infant political organisation must adopt majority-voting systems, as has occurred with some parties' online polls.[45] Applications exist for consensus-driven, moderated debates. Entire new structures can be created, too, with any inbuilt modifications desired. Minority groups can be represented, constitutional changes could require two-thirds majorities.

The democracy creed is a driving principle of recent political change. Its re-manifestation is not, however, set in concrete, and each of the four parties studied have differed in their approaches.

[45]https://www.opendemocracy.net/can-europe-make-it/lorenzo-del-savio-matteo-mameli/antirepresentative-democracy-how-to-understand-fi

7

An analysis of four political parties

Movimento 5 Stelle

Applying e-democracy to find practical solutions to current problems

The ruling coalition in Italy is known as the Government of Change and has been in power since June 2018. The senior party is the Five Stars Movement, which won around 32% of the popular vote in both chambers of parliament. Other parties formed coalitions to run in elections, meaning Five Stars alone earned every one of its votes, and is thus perhaps the most popular single political entity in Italy. It shares government with Lega Nord, a right-wing and regionalist party.

"Movement" applies to Five Stars much more than "party". There is no fixed loyalty to pre-existing political ideologies or traditional intricate hierarchies. Policies are formed, bottom-up, by a large group of members who engage in discussions online. As Corrado Poli, an academic and author who has studied Five Stars, wrote for Radix in March 2018: *"The founders of Five Stars' politics believe that their role is not to propose ideas and programmes, but to represent what the people communicate."*[46]

---

[46] C. Poli, 'Five Stars', *Radix*, https://radix.org.uk/five-stars-dreaming-radically-new-politics/

By using the internet, Five Stars has accumulated a large sweep of supporters across the country who wish to have their voices heard and translated into policy. The aim, in effect, is to apply e-democracy to provide practical solutions for current problems.

Early Beginnings

Although qualifying as an insurgent political party, the Five Stars Movement's rise was not as sudden and meteoric as it might at first seem. Its original base were fans of an established – but not establish*ment* – comedian called Beppe Grillo. An outspoken critic of Italian politics during his sets, Grillo had even been banned from television in the 1980s – proof positive of his anti-establishment credentials.

In 2005, Grillo suggested that his audiences should come together, away from his performances. Using the online website *Meetup*, members held discussion groups on a variety of topics. Joining forces with like-minded people appealed, and these groups became known as the "40 Friends of Beppe Grillo".

From these beginnings, the movement spread. Beppe Grillo fans became supporters of a new political agitation. In 2007, *Vaffanculo* Days (translated as "Fuck-Off Days") were held in different cities, with the aim of accruing signatures for a petition banning parliamentary candidates who have criminal convictions or who have already served two terms in office. They received hundreds of thousands of signatures. In 2008, the movement created civic lists of candidates to run in the Italian local elections. In September the following year, a national movement was announced in Milan, marking the official birth date of the Five Stars Movement.

Internet Outreach

It still took nearly nine years to reach government, but it did so as the largest single party in the popular vote. Beppe Grillo remained the central lynchpin which drew these new activists together. His blog, beppegrillo.it, was enormously popular and allowed this new political stars to convey his views directly to the people, at any time he saw fit. This has translated into a large youth base of supporters, whose understanding and use of the internet gives them optimal access.[47]

For Poli, Grillo was the speaker, the public face, of the movement, but Five Stars is not the same as his one-man shows. Early this year, an official *Blog delle Stelle* was created, to function as a mouthpiece for the wider circle of Five Stars leaders. These leaders included Gianroberto Casaleggio, whose consultancy, Casaleggio Associati, run since his death by his son, Davide Casaleggio, manages Five Stars' internet output.[48]

And there is a lot of it. According to Buzzfeed reporting from 2016, the company's network includes *TzeTze* and *La Cosa*, popular news sites, and even topic-specific websites like the health-focused *La Fucina*. Such sites have received heavy criticism and epithets like fake news, but there is little denying their effeciveness.

It is difficult to confirm the number of visitors to these sites; helpfully, Facebook interaction is easier to track. One video post claiming the existence of a US-Turkey conspiracy to prevent Russia from fighting ISIS received 1.3 million views. This might be a particularly high exception, but similar patterns of cross-pollination between social media sites and Casaleggio sites are common.[49] The fantastical content of

---

[47] C. Poli, 'Five Stars', *Radix*, https://radix.org.uk/five-stars-dreaming-radically-new-politics/

[48] J. Politi, H. Roberts, 'Five Star Movement', *Financial Times*, www.ft.com/content/546be098-989f-11e7-a652-cde3f882dd7b, 17/09/2017

[49] A. Nardelli, C. Silverman, 'Italy's Most Popular Political Party', *Buzzfeed News*, www.buzzfeed.com/albertonardelli/italys-most-popular-political-party-is-leading-europe-in-fak

these stories may be part of their attraction. But the sophistication of this network and the tactics used to attract readers – which presumably often translates to voters – are worthy of attention.

New Alternative to Stale Status Quo

Not only does Five Stars encourage close interaction and engagement with activists, but it also chimes with a central theme of anti-establishmentarianism.

Grillo had railed against status quo politicians for decades, and his "Clean Parliament" initiative of the 2000s encapsulated a mood of distrust surrounding the contemporary political system. For many years, the Five Stars movement purposely shunned the mainstream or official media, refusing to give interviews to newspapers or appear on talk-shows.[50] This rule was relaxed after the election of Five Stars candidates into the Chamber of Deputies, but Five Stars' own media channels are still their prized form of communication. Luigi di Maio, for example, used the *Blog delle Stelle* to call those who opposed the government's controversial budget plans as "enemies of Italy".[51] Although one of the most powerful people of the state, di Maio remains in contact with followers directly. In the case of the Five Stars Movement, symbiosis exists between opinions and the way they are conveyed. An insurgent political body must do things differently.

Another example of activists' proficiency in publicity and persuasion are the Vaffanculo Days, or V-Days, from early-on

[50] C. Poli, 'Five Stars', *Radix*, https://radix.org.uk/five-stars-dreaming-radically-new-politics/

[51] A. Nardelli, 'As Italy's Nationalist Government Rises in Popularity', *Buzzfeed News*,

www.buzzfeednews.com/article/albertonardelli/luigi-di-maio-matteo-salvini-donald-trump; www.ilblogdellestelle.it/2018/09/i_nemici_dellitalia.html

in the movement's history. Summing up a mood of disenchantment via use of profanity, the 'V' also conjures up positivist and evocative associations from Julius Caesar's triumphant "veni, vidi, vici", to the film *V for Vendetta*, which depicts a victorious overthrow of a corrupt political system.

But perhaps above all it represented the number 5, for the titular stars: water, environment, transport, connectivity and development.[52] These wide-ranging and non-specific terms are perhaps the flip-side of the coin for an anti-establishment campaign. In turn, they attract diverse voters. Poli adds that many Five Stars members are middle class and educated, but find themselves disenchanted by the lack of suitable jobs for them.[53] Five Stars was able to pick up these votes, including those from previous voting abstainers.

Internet Organisation

The genesis of Five Stars justifies its claim to be a *movimento* and not a traditional party. The banner, after all, is too wide to fit into the traditional party restrictions of an ideology. Members join by signing up to *Rousseau*, an online platform which hosts discussions of Five Stars policies alongside primary elections of Five Stars candidates. Echoing Jean-Jacques Rousseau's concept of the general will, this aims to be direct democracy in action.[54]

As of March 2017, the platform was reported to have 140,000 members, offering 80,000 amendments and

[52] C. Bickerton, 'The Five Star Movement', *LSE*, http://blogs.lse.ac.uk/europpblog/2018/05/24/the-five-star-movement-and-the-rise-of-techno-populist-parties/

[53] C. Poli, 'Five Stars', *Radix*, https://radix.org.uk/five-stars-dreaming-radically-new-politics/

[54] J. Politi, H. Roberts, 'Five Star Movement', *Financial Times*, www.ft.com/content/546be098-989f-11e7-a652-cde3f882dd7b, 17/09/2017

suggestions to 250 policy proposals given by Five Stars deputies, regional representatives and EU politicians.[55] Votes are taken on key debates. Candidates post CVs and videos before Rousseau members vote on who runs for political office.[56] A company called DNV is supposed to certify the votes.[57] A tool called *Lex Iscritti* reportedly allows members to write potential policies themselves. There are even tutorials posted to explain how the Italian political system works for the uninitiated. In theory, Five Stars becomes a conduit for its members' voices, and thus a whole new way of doing politics.[58]

The platform is not open source, and thus the people who join are screened and the possibility of hijacking is avoided.[59] This does create costs, but nothing, Five Stars assures us, like the overheads of traditional parties. Supporters can even donate through *Rousseau* – according to Davide Casaleggio, most of the movement's funding comes in this form of €30 micro-donations.[60] Further revenue appears to come in from Google Ads and the like, which run on the Casaleggio Associati network. Big sponsors include brands like Sky and Durex,

[55] These figures were given by Davide Casaleggio, however, and are therefore not independent

[56] D. Casaleggio, 'How Italians Learned to Govern Themselves Through Technology', *Huffpost*, www.huffingtonpost.com/entry/five-star-movement-internet_us_58cb008ae4b0be71dcf3048d?guccounter=1

[57] J. Politi, H. Roberts, 'Five Star Movement', *Financial Times*, www.ft.com/content/546be098-989f-11e7-a652-cde3f882dd7b, 17/09/2017

[58] D. Casaleggio, 'How Italians Learned to Govern Themselves Through Technology', *Huffpost*, www.huffingtonpost.com/entry/five-star-movement-internet_us_58cb008ae4b0be71dcf3048d?guccounter=1

[59] J. Politi, H. Roberts, 'Five Star Movement', *Financial Times*, www.ft.com/content/546be098-989f-11e7-a652-cde3f882dd7b, 17/09/2017

[60] D. Casaleggio, 'How Italians Learned to Govern Themselves Through Technology', *Huffpost*, www.huffingtonpost.com/entry/five-star-movement-internet_us_58cb008ae4b0be71dcf3048d?guccounter=1

although, as the *Financial Times* reports, the exact amount generated is unclear.[61] Not only is the net a way to spread your message at low cost, it can even be used to make surplus.

Downsides and warnings

The Five Stars Movement has been the target of some important criticism.

Despite an intended focus on people-power, Five Stars nurtures a core in the form of Casaleggio Associati. The firm runs both the movement's media network and the *Rousseau* platform. One issue with the instant access of the internet is that it forms a centralised media controlled by an elite. Davide Casaleggio's political beliefs are undeclared, but that doesn't assuage fears that he has a direct line to many people's ears, without external moderation or divergent opinion.[62]

A related point is self-imposed segregation these online platforms facilitate. Thanks to the internet, Poli notes, "we are much more provincial than when we lived in a small village". People sign up under the influence of blogs and Beppe Grillo; they do not always find challenges to their views on *Rousseau*. The thematic discussion platforms – in existence since the original 40 Friends of Beppe Grillo – encourage narrow focus on single-issues. A holistic and rounded understanding of broad needs might be lost.

There is a lack of a geographic "home" for Five Stars. In traditional – constituency-based – parties, activists interact with people in their local area. Geographic divisions of class and race exist, but political views may be more dispersed. People do not engage with their local communities and, as a

[61] J. Politi, H. Roberts, 'Five Star Movement', *Financial Times*, www.ft.com/content/546be098-989f-11e7-a652-cde3f882dd7b, 17/09/2017

[62] J. Politi, H. Roberts, 'Five Star Movement', *Financial Times*, www.ft.com/content/546be098-989f-11e7-a652-cde3f882dd7b, 17/09/2017

result, Five Stars hardly participates in local elections.[63] Any movement which wishes to encourage honest civic engagement should perhaps develop countermeasures to avoid these outcomes.

On Balance ...

... Five Stars is far from an ideal model of modern political parties. It originated with a reformist agenda but is in danger of being corrupted by the shadowy machinations behind the scenes.

Rousseau is an extreme and exciting innovation – but even without Casaleggio Associati's unsettling influences, the consequences of such direct democracy need to be considered carefully.

Five Stars is undoubtedly ambitious and highly innovative, building its own platforms and sites, with a sustained readership. If others can create these online spaces, hopefully without shutting users off from other media, then they should be in a strong position electorally.

The scale of Five Stars' operation, and its clever marketing make it an impressive organisation. The trick is to replicate its winning strategies without fuelling its more unnerving aspects. Unfortunately, the downsides might be inextricable from Five Stars' model of success.

La République En Marche!

New blood, new methods, and a fresh start for France – helped by an opponent most voters could not stomach

From the time of its inception to the Presidential election, *La République En Marche* had existed for just over one year.

---

[63] C. Poli, 'Five Stars', *Radix*, https://radix.org.uk/five-stars-dreaming-radically-new-politics/

Founded by Emmanuel Macron, a strange mix of former investment banker and Socialist government minister, this party-cum-movement presented itself as an alternative to the status-quo politics, amidst a climate of widespread dissatisfaction.

Mirroring Macron's own paradoxical career, En Marche is neither left nor right in any recognisable way. Nicolas Firzli, director of the World Pensions Forum, characterises Macron as a statist technocrat and 'liberal moderniser'. But, above all, *En Marche* received support for the professed principles and values it seemed to embody. Facing the popularity of Marine Le Pen's Front National, a right-wing nationalist party, *En Marche* and Macron stood for internationalism, globalisation and the future as opposed to a return to a mythical past.[64]

The first round of the 2017 Presidential election saw Emmanuel Macron come first, with nearly a million more votes than Marine Le Pen, François Fillon of the Republicans and Jean-Luc Mélenchon of *La France Insoumise*. Some have seen this as a relatively weak turnout for Macron, though given *En Marche*'s young age, he does seem to have convinced a large number of people to drop previous allegiances in a very short time.

In the second round, people united against Le Pen; the final vote share for 66.1 per cent against 33.9 per cent in Macron's favour.

The following elections to the National Assembly secured a 350-seat majority (out of 577 seats) for *En Marche*, in alliance with the smaller, more traditional centrist *MoDem* (remnants of provincialist Catholic centre-right parties once popular in Western France, Alsace and parts of the Pyrenees).

---

[64] A. Nossiter, 'Why Macron Won', *The New York Times*,
https://www.nytimes.com/2017/05/07/world/europe/why-macron-won-france.html

Armed with this new balanced support, Macron had been pushing forward with his widespread, neoliberal-inspired economic reforms for over a year, when, seemingly all of a sudden, he was faced with the *Gilets Jaunes'* ("Yellow Vests") Winter of Discontent marked by unending, violent demonstrations across the country and, in some instances, full-scale urban riots spilling over into the fashionable neighbourhoods of Paris, Bordeaux and Montpelier, strongholds of the Macronist bourgeoisie.[65]

Surprising Change

La République En Marche makes most sense with France's presidential system in mind. When Emmanuel Macron formally announced the creation of *En Marche* in his hometown of Amiens in April 2016, he was a recognised figure as former Minister for the Economy, Industry and Digital Affairs in Francois Hollande's cabinet. With the latter's unpopularity, however, Macron judged he could not succeed him whilst in the *Parti Socialiste*. A new base of support needed to arise – and this was the *raison d'etre* of *En Marche*.

Joining was easy and accessible – no fee, quick online sign-up, and the ability to join whilst still being a member of another party.[66] This revolution in French politics was thus in some ways unexpected, stemming from the needs of a candidate in a race which elects only one person.

Yet revolution was indeed what resulted from Macron's plan for a new political organisation. The *En Marche* website

---

[65] These tragic events are still unfolding as we write these lines and it remains to be seen whether Macron's 'Grand National Debate' will quench their fury...

[66] From interviews

received 30,000 registrations in the first few weeks.[67] As much as €6.5 million was collected from individual donations during the presidential campaign.[68] After signing up – with a few personal details and agreement to a charter of values – any member could then set-up a local committee. As with volunteer self-registration, these committees have a lot of autonomy to plan their own activities. This fit with the idea of a civic society movement and brought like-minded constituents and neighbours together.

Aside from their own page of the *En Marche* website to direct new recruits, and a suggestion pack of potential activities or debate topics, the committees were independent.[69] Around 4,000 existed at the time of the National Assembly elections.[70] This was complemented by the make-up of *En Marche* politicians: half of *En Marche* ministers are new to politics, whilst 30 per cent of *En Marche* representatives in the National Assembly had never sought office before and 30 per cent had only been involved in local politics. No previously-existing politicians could create local committees, either – new, fresh blood, excited by Macron, was needed.[71]

[67] C. O'Brien, 'Meet the presidential candidate', *Venturebeat*, https://venturebeat.com/2017/01/08/meet-the-french-presidential-candidate-whos-using-the-internet-to-reinvent-politics/

[68] P. Block, 'The new French revolution', *New Statesman*, https://www.newstatesman.com/culture/2017/06/new-french-revolution-how-en-marche-disrupted-politics

[69] From interviews

[70] P. Block, 'The new French revolution', *New Statesman*, www.newstatesman.com/culture/2017/06/new-french-revolution-how-en-marche-disrupted-politics

[71] From interviews

In an interview with the author right before the start of the Yellow Vests demonstrations, Firzli, stressed that the true size of *La République En Marche*'s (LREM) electoral base has been exaggerated. This excited, fresh blood which supports Macron's political convictions are actually a very small social set positioned precisely at the crossroads where higher education, finance, and high-tech meet.

True fans are still active – recent battles between Macron and provincial politicians over housing tax saw *En Marche* activists publish lists of around 6,000 mayors who increased the tax contrary to the President's will.[72] But others have left after being surprised by the sudden enforcement of old-fashioned hierarchical rules by the powers that be at *En Marche*'s Parisian headquarters.

The long-term outcomes of this post-election change have yet to be seen, but the unfolding Yellow Vests crisis, which some LREM ministers initially seemed content to let fester, combined with reform fatigue among large sections of the lower-middle-class at home and increasing scepticism in Brussels and Berlin regarding Macron's euphoric Europhilia, may well force the President and his core-followers to curb their reformist zeal: the European parliamentary elections of 24-26 May 2019 may well constitute a life-or-death test for LREM.

Building a Platform

Nevertheless, journalists such as Yann L'Hénoret, who directed a Netflix documentary on Macron, have commented

[72]https://www.ft.com/content/e20122a8-d1ef-11e8-a9f2-7574db66bcd5?accessToken=zwAAAWbP0mSgkdPiASKo0e8R6NOp8nV022a81Q.MEUCIQDck2-kh3jVmtjcTxB0z3c-9AVUhWvzkuFl-4Z65Ix6QQIgAboCML8aPCrJPCgVzqtGUt7Z3Xe6902eR1L9gVZxnZU&sharetype=gift

on Macron's collaborative spirit as everyone could give their own view before he came to a final decision.[73]

In this vein, perhaps, Macron undertook an ambitious, large-scale project previously unheard of in France, during the months before the election. *La Grande Marche* involved a mass door-knocking operation to gather data on what the French public thought were the next steps needed in their country's future.

France is privacy-conscious; parties cannot even copy voting records. Liegey Muller Pons (LMP) is a Paris-based firm formed by three former Obama volunteers. What they learnt from the US campaigns was the utility of data – which helped target most-likely voters for contact and advertising.

From online registrations, LMP turned about 5,000 signatories into *En Marche* volunteers, gave them basic interviewing tips and management skills, and set them to work. An app was developed which made data-collection as easy as possible via the use of keywords. For instance, volunteers could ask the question "what doesn't work in France?". If the interviewee commented on their children's schooling, the keyword "education" would be tapped. Over three months, volunteers spoke to 100,000 people and filled out 25,000 questionnaires.[74]

LREM on the whole, shuns traditional left-right ideological spectrums.[75] Macron has been both banker and socialist, but perhaps "technocrat" suits him best. His reformist agenda

[73] P. Block, 'The new French revolution', *New Statesman*, www.newstatesman.com/culture/2017/06/new-french-revolution-how-en-marche-disrupted-politics

[74] C. O'Brien, 'Meet the presidential candidate', *Venturebeat*, https://venturebeat.com/2017/01/08/meet-the-french-presidential-candidate-whos-using-the-internet-to-reinvent-politics/

[75] From interviews

seems to speak to this desire to fix problems but avoid utopian five-year plans.[76] If there is one constant in Macron's vision, it may well be the promises of tech-nation exceptionalism.

Technology heavily intertwined with door-knocking in Macron's election run. Drawing from the conversations of *La Grande Marche*, the data analyst firm Proxem determined the most common themes of the responses and how strongly the interviewees felt about each of them. Macron then delivered his diagnostic on the state of the nation in three public meetings, three hours each, live-streamed across the internet.

"Family" and "social protection" were hot-button issues, with "solidarity" and "integrity" as important values.[77] When Macron unveiled his platform, only two months before the first vote, his policies reflected what he had heard from the public.[78] His liberalism, for instance, is tempered with protections like the Posted Workers' Directive, in which employees of foreign firms must be paid at the same rates as their host communities and thus avoiding undercutting local workers.[79]

Ultimately, though, the 2017 French elections were a battle of values.[80] In Spring 2017, Le Pen was rising in the polls, and the *Parti socialiste* was badly damaged by distaste for

[76] E. Halls, 'Emmanuel Macron says France needs a King', *GQ*,

www.gq-magazine.co.uk/article/emmanuel-macron-policies-beliefs-philosophy

[77] C. O'Brien, 'Meet the presidential candidate', *Venturebeat*, https://venturebeat.com/2017/01/08/meet-the-french-presidential-candidate-whos-using-the-internet-to-reinvent-politics/

[78] From interviews

[79] From interviews p.9

[80] A. Nossiter, 'Why Macron Won', *The New York Times*, https://www.nytimes.com/2017/05/07/world/europe/why-macron-won-france.html

Hollande. It is unsurprising that most left-leaning votes went to Macron as the alternative to destabilisation. But Macron courted the right, too, with his Jeanne d'Arc speech in Rouen, which invoked an appealing narrative of one person's crusade from the provinces to the Champs-Elysées, in order to save the country.[81]

The one thing everyone agreed on, it seems, was the need for change (80% in a *Liberation/ViaVoice* poll noted support for "a strong and clear cut from the politics of the last years").[82] Le Pen and Mélenchon were both politicians who argued for large-scale shake-ups but Macron was the one who argued for change in a "constructive" manner – not to revert to a non-globalised former world, but to change the world as it was.[83]

Modern marketing to suit modern politics

Perhaps to underline that he wanted no part in the staid traditional political fights, Macron avoided reacting to the other candidates. For any negative campaigning deemed necessary, "Team Macron" took over.[84] Instead, Emmanuel Macron chose to speak directly to voters over the internet and far from traditional outlet intermediaries. His campaign announcement took place at a community meeting, not, as usual, a press conference.[85] This was complemented by a

---

[81] From interviews p.16

[82] From interviews

[83] From interviews

[84] From interviews

[85] From interviews

personal blog post.[86] French law bans paid advertising, but Facebook pages offered a free way to reach plenty of people. Discussions were live-streamed and long adverts posted.[87]

Technology offered a divide-and-conquer approach to the *En Marche* campaign. Whilst the younger generations were being reached via social media sites, *En Marche* used the three minutes of television time given by electoral regulations in the last two weeks to talk to the older public who still watch.[88] Meanwhile, Sunday Lunch Times Initiatives were created to educate younger supporters about political issues in order to talk about them at home. Some even included scripts.[89]

The prongs of attack were endless: for the apolitical, Macron gave interviews to gossip magazines and local newspapers in efforts to reach them.[90]

Conclusion

Despite an unprecedented rise, and a majority in the National Assembly, Macron continues to battle on all fronts, whilst opinion polls indicate an unfavourable turn in public attitude. This is an inevitable readjustment in which the Macronist river is simply returning to its normal, gently flowing level.

The truth is, Macron owes a debt to Le Pen, who remained a pill the majority of French citizens found impossible to swallow. *En Marche* has a lot of work to do if it wants to thrive

[86] C. O'Brien, 'Meet the presidential candidate', *Venturebeat*, https://venturebeat.com/2017/01/08/meet-the-french-presidential-candidate-whos-using-the-internet-to-reinvent-politics/

[87] From interviews

[88] From interviews

[89] From interviews

[90] From interviews

in the future and not be a second choice for voters worried their preferred candidates will not stop the far-right. With this in doubt, *En Marche*'s small successes are the most fruitful to study. Its quick growth rate through the structure of a non-traditional movement, and its intelligent marketing methods, deserve appreciation.

The liberal-idealist civic engagement of *La Grande Marche* combined with the coldly professional, e-marketing-savvy analysis of data was a tricky balance to maintain over a long period of time. It remains to be seen whether these factors can be replicated in another context, or even in France itself by 2022 ... *'À qui il a été beaucoup donné, il sera beaucoup demandé'* says an ancient Gallic proverb (To whom much is given, much will be demanded).

Having given *En Marche* "a lot" back in 2017, French voters may be inclined to be far less generous next time around – unless the President can deliver rapidly on the disparate, burgeoning expectations of his rebellious people.

Liberal Party of Canada

Turning conventional wisdom on its head

Far from being a new political force, the Liberals were established in 1867 and governed Canada for around 70 years during the 20th century. In 2011, however, the Liberal Party was in tatters, sinking to third-place position behind the New Democratic Party and the Conservatives. Which makes the gaining of 148 seats and a Commons majority of 14 in the 2015 federal election even more surprising.

In contrast with Five Star, En Marche and Podemos, the Liberal Party of Canada is a traditional political organisation. Its victory in 2015 was perhaps more traditional too. "Tools don't win campaigns," comments Tom Pitfield, the Liberals' Chief Digital Strategist – policies, authenticity and a good leader do. The Liberals certainly show that a revitalised centrist-leaning force can be achieved with the down-to-earth Canadian attitude.

New Leader, New Direction

Justin Trudeau, revered across the globe for his relaxed charm and shiny hair, gained similar admiration from his fellow Canadians.

To win elections, however, he had to command a deeper appeal. Famous because of his father, Pierre Trudeau, Canadian Prime Minister in the late '70s and early '80s, Justin had to shake off an image of entitlement and privilege.

According to *Maclean's*, a current affairs magazine, he more than stepped up to the task. A poor debater at first, described by a campaign staffer as "overly theatrical", he underwent copious practice and took on board constructive criticism.[91]

As in the UK, the Prime Minister is the leader of the largest party in the House of Commons. And like the presidentialisation of UK leaders such as Tony Blair, each party's leader has a huge impact on public support. The regeneration of Trudeau's image in turn helped regenerate the party.

Trudeau's draw for voters will be discussed more below, but, like the hair, it should not turn our attention from his impact on his own party.

As leader, the buck stops with him. But Trudeau made sure he made use of other voices. In particular, he consulted the experts. His economic advisory committee included Larry Summers, Obama's economic adviser, and David Dodge, formerly Governor of the Bank of Canada. It was this

---

[91] P. Wells, 'The making of a prime minister', *Maclean's*, http://site.macleans.ca/longform/trudeau/index.html

committee that came up with a winning pledge of short-term deficit spending channelled into infrastructure investment.

For Trudeau, listening to experts doesn't equate with ignoring voters. Internal polls in 2014 put belief in a "time for a change" 20 points higher than three years previously, which bolstered confidence in the deficit-spending plan.[92]

Additionally, Canadian politicians benefit from the experience of provinces. If the Liberal Association of New Brunswick could win a majority in that province's legislature whilst supporting an increased marginal tax rate on high incomes, then perhaps the federal Liberals could too.[93]

In essence, this was top-down leadership, but leadership in conference. Trudeau drew on the resources available to him in a way that is miles away from Trump's style, and worthy of recognition.

Bottom-Up - Grassroots Engagement

Trudeau's Liberals also sought engagement of a wider kind away from the circle of advisors.

In Spring 2014, the party hired Hilary Leftick as volunteer mobilisation officer. She instantly established door-knocking as a top priority. In October, the first Day of Action was held targeting 100 ridings (constituencies). On one weekend in June 2015, there were volunteers out in every riding. This was unprecedented in Canada, where door-knocking only occurred

[92] P. Wells, 'The making of a prime minister', *Maclean's*, http://site.macleans.ca/longform/trudeau/index.html

[93] D. Butler, 'Why the Liberals embraced deficits', *Ottawa Citizen*, https://ottawacitizen.com/news/politics/why-the-liberals-embraced-deficits-to-fix-the-economy-and-win-an-election; G. McGregor, 'Former Martin aide used provincial campaigns to lay out the road map to Trudeau's victory', *Ottawa Citizen*, https://ottawacitizen.com/news/politics/former-martin-aide-used-provincial-campaigns-to-lay-out-the-road-map-to-trudeaus-victory

during campaign weeks at the same time as keen Liberal supporters spent time with each other at wine and cheese fundraisers.[94]

Here, the federals could again learn from the provincials in Ontario, where volunteers of the local Liberal Party from Kathleen Wynne's successful 2013 leadership reassembled for the federal election. This did three things. First, lessons learnt from Wynne's campaign could be used for the federal campaign. And secondly, it activated and tapped the energy of supporters.[95]

The newly-motivated rank-and-file of the Liberal Party is Chief 2015 Campaign Advisor Katie Telford's prize possession. At the party's 2016 convention, she spoke about the 80,000 volunteers who made 12 million door-knocks and phone calls.[96] That's 12 million outreaches to a population of 35 million – a sizeable chunk. By using volunteers, the party also saved an estimated CAN$3 million. This advantage is trickier for parties like the NDP, whose links to unions does not engender the same loyalty seen in Liberal volunteers.[97] This is the new status-quo - door-knocking continued after the election, encouraged by the 4,000 volunteers who signed up *after* the election.[98]

[94] P. Wells, 'The making of a prime minister', *Maclean's*, http://site.macleans.ca/longform/trudeau/index.html

[95] G. McGregor, 'Former Martin aide used provincial campaigns to lay out the road map to Trudeau's victory', *Ottawa Citizen*, https://ottawacitizen.com/news/politics/former-martin-aide-used-provincial-campaigns-to-lay-out-the-road-map-to-trudeaus-victory

[96] K. Telford, '2016 Liberal Convention', *CPAC*, www.youtube.com/watch?v=tbRWkz4zLtE

[97] P. Wells, 'The making of a prime minister', *Maclean's*, http://site.macleans.ca/longform/trudeau/index.html

[98] M. Hemmadi, 'Trudeau's chief of staff', *Maclean's*, https://www.macleans.ca/politics/ottawa/trudeaus-chief-of-staff-katie-telford-on-

'...And Outward' - Public Connection

It is clear that the Liberals regard volunteer outreach as essential to the 2015 win. But the party, the most traditional under review, is also well-versed in more modern forms of campaigning.

Reporter Susan Delacourt has written extensively about the Liberal's use of data. Some of this was collected from door-knock conversations, but most of it was from online platforms, on which people voluntarily share where they live, who they are friends with and what they do with their time. All this was put into what was called The Console, a database which ranked ridings in order of how winnable they were. Alongside individual voters themselves scored from 1 (no-use bothering) to 10 (die-hard Liberal).

This was a huge innovation on previous election campaigns, where the Liberals' understanding of their voters "resembled a phone directory".[99] The Conservatives have similar data resources, which they used to identify sources of funds.[100] What worked for the Liberals was targeting marketing materials to specific social media users and ridings. Data was considered so highly in this campaign that Trudeau visited areas on the condition that event organisers gathered contact information from attendees.[101] This, in turn, drew

life-inside-the-pmo/; K. Telford, '2016 Liberal Convention', *CPAC*, www.youtube.com/watch?v=tbRWkz4zLtE

[99] S. Delacourt, 'Team Trudeau and the Liberal's Facebook conundrum', *iPolitics*, https://ipolitics.ca/2018/03/21/team-trudeau-and-the-liberals-facebook-conundrum

[100] S. Delacourt,, 'The permanent campaign', *The Star*, www.thestar.com/news/insight/2015/06/05/the-permanent-campaign-is-now-a-canadian-institution-delacourt.html

[101] S. Delacourt, 'Q&A', *Vancouver Sun*, https://vancouversun.com/entertainment/books/q-and-a-susan-delacourt

more in – around half the people who attended rallies were invited through email and social media accounts.[102]

Facebook, in particular, has the ideal apparatus. Trudeau launched the entire Liberal campaign platform from a town hall which was streamed live over Facebook. He answered questions that users posted as they came in.[103] Online adverts were posted into individual's walls, whilst Twitter and Instagram accounts remain active.[104]

As Facebook's youth membership wanes, it remains integral to follow this new generation onto the new platforms. Plurality of marketing material needs to be deployed, and also changed constantly to keep up with the next talking-points. New structures for communication breeds new styles. Facebook is for friends – Trudeau relaxed into this sense of the familiar when he took part in the platform's 60-Second Challenge, answering rapid-fire questions about his personal life. Knowing his favourite food, or how many times his children have watched *Frozen,* doesn't seem directly connected to persuading voters to make him Prime Minister. But it does respond to the demands of relatability and authenticity, a value which Pitfield stresses.[105]

Connection with voters is crucial. Stephen Harper, Canadian PM leading the Conservatives in 2015, tried to play

[102] S. Delacourt, 'Team Trudeau and the Liberal's Facebook conundrum', *iPolitics*, https://ipolitics.ca/2018/03/21/team-trudeau-and-the-liberals-facebook-conundrum

[103] K. Chan, 'Facebook and the Federal Election: A New Platform for Civic Engagement', *Policy Magazine*, http://policymagazine.ca/pdf/16/PolicyMagazineNovemberDecember-2015-Chan.pdf

[104] S. Delacourt, 'Team Trudeau and the Liberal's Facebook conundrum', *iPolitics*, https://ipolitics.ca/2018/03/21/team-trudeau-and-the-liberals-facebook-conundrum

[105] K. Chan, 'Facebook and the Federal Election: A New Platform for Civic Engagement', *Policy Magazine*, http://policymagazine.ca/pdf/16/PolicyMagazineNovemberDecember-2015-Chan.pdf

on his leadership qualities. But perhaps "leader" now sounds too distant.

Old-Fashioned Hope

In the wake of the Cambridge Analytica scandal this year, data has become a blighted term for political organisations. Helpful, then, that Tom Pitfield asserts the importance of a different marketing strategy – a fundamental narrative at the heart of the party's campaign.

The Chief Digital Strategist worked on the Obama campaign, and narrative is something often referred to by the former US President. We "have to understand what is motivating them", Pitfield says, referring to voters, and use this to engage people. Trudeau made a lot of the term "sunny ways". This was a quote from a former Liberal leader, Sir Wilfrid Laurier, back in 1895, grounding the 2015 campaign in over one hundred years of history.[106]

The official slogan of the campaign was "Real Change", one which focuses on the future. A vision of hope was thus threaded from past to future, complemented by emphasis on unity and Canadian pride. As Gerald Butts, a top campaign advisor, said in Delacourt's book *Shopping for Votes*, digital platforms are not simply for dividing voters and conquering them. They can be used to bring people together.[107]

Different

In one memorable moment from the 2015 election, the Liberal campaign turned conventional wisdom on its head.

[106] 'The "Sunny Way", *Liberal*, www.liberal.ca/the-sunny-way/

[107] S. Delacourt, 'Q&A', *Vancouver Sun*,
https://vancouversun.com/entertainment/books/q-and-a-susan-delacourt

A Conservative attack-ad had labelled Trudeau as "not ready", supplementing Stephen Harper's argument emphasising his leadership experience. The Liberals shocked almost everyone when they acknowledged this ad – and turned it around. "Stephen Harper says I'm not ready", Trudeau notes; but he isn't ready "to watch hard-working Canadians lose jobs". He's bolder than that, ready "to do what my opponents won't: ask our wealthiest to pay more tax, so our middle class can pay less".[108] The Liberals weren't trying to outrun Harper on his own ground – Trudeau could never claim to have the same experience. Instead, they re-drew the battle lines and added their own unique voice.

This is clear with regard to the deficit question. Both the Conservative and the NDP argued for balanced budgets – making the Liberal's stance different and distinct. This book does not mean to appraise policies or ideologies themselves. What is clear, though, is that highlighting a party's difference is good marketing. In a political climate where the public uses elections and referendums to voice its discontent with the status quo, standing out attracts these votes.

In Pitfield's view, Trudeau's rebuttal ad was popular because it suggested the Liberals were tired with how the mass media shaped the political debate. The public agreed. The Liberal Party shows that you can be bold, even populist, without descending into chaos.

Conclusion

The next Canadian federal election is scheduled for 2019, and with four years in government, the Liberal Party's narrative has changed. Political run-ins over a carbon tax, and a

---

[108] P. Wells, 'The making of a prime minister', *Maclean's*, http://site.macleans.ca/longform/trudeau/index.html; 'New Liberal Ad: Justin Says Justin Is Ready', *FactPointVideo*, www.youtube.com/watch?v=1gFyv2M84nl

misjudged trip to India, have garnered bad press.[109] They are no longer the alternative. Pitfield says the Liberals can now shout about responsible leadership, which was what Stephen Harper used to campaign on. Nonetheless, Trudeau does indeed illustrate the power of a good leader to transform a party. The Liberal's use of data and door-knocking brought the federal party into its 21st-century version, with electoral dividends.

This is not revolutionary, nor nearly as radical as Five Stars' innovations and yet, it still worked.

Podemos

Channeling street anger and political agitation into electoral success by knowing its audience

On the 15 May 2011, people across dozens of Spanish cities held protests against the austerity measures of the Socialist Workers' Party government in response to the Eurozone crisis. Around 6 to 8.5 million protestors were counted over the wave of demonstrations that spring, all wishing to have their voices heard in the local, regional and even general elections held that year.[110]

Many formed political bodies in the months and years which followed, of which Podemos was one. Aware of the emphasis placed on people-power in the anti-austerity movement, the founders of Podemos understood that a similar openness was needed in a new electoral movement. An initial application for joint open primaries with the pre-existing *Izquierda Unida* (United Left) was rejected, and thus

---

[109] J. Geddes, 'Election 2019: The battle lines are already drawn', *Maclean's*, www.macleans.ca/politics/ottawa/election-2019-the-battle-lines-are-already-drawn

[110] 'Más de seis millones de españoles han participado en el Movimiento 15M', *RTVE*, www.rtve.es/noticias/20110806/mas-seis-millones-espanoles-han-participado-movimiento-15m/452598.shtml

Podemos was officially inaugurated in Madrid, on 17 January 2014.

At the EU elections of 2014, just 4 months later, Podemos won 8 per cent of the vote, enough to elect five MEPs. It reached 21 per cent of the vote at the 2015 general election, marking an end to the two-party politics that had dominated Spain since the death of Franco.

Podemos often forms alliances with other parties it shares ideologies with – in this way Podemos members support the mayors of Barcelona and Madrid. In the 2016 general election, Podemos formed alliances with several other left-wing and regional parties to receive 21 per cent of the vote. In 2018, Podemos was called upon to sign a budget pact with the PSOE, and, according to *El Pais*, is expecting to govern in a coalition in 2020.[111]

The New Democracy

The *15-M movement*, as the protests are known, has become a watershed moment in Spain's history. Hit with 20 per cent unemployment, 40 per cent amongst young people, there was a keen belief that the political elite did not care about the population it was governing.[112] Podemos attempts to reflect this demand for a new democracy with the way it organizes itself. Its website, for instance, publishes an audit of all spending inside the organisation.[113] Party lists are used in Spain's electoral system and Podemos' offerings are called

[111] J. Macros, A. Macros, 'Spain's Podemos', *El Pais*, https://elpais.com/elpais/2018/10/16/inenglish/1539692544_763322.html?rel=str_a rticulo#1540831123832

[112] D. Beas, 'How Spain's 15-M movement is redefining politics', *Guardian*, www.theguardian.com/commentisfree/2011/oct/15/spain-15-m-movement-activism

[113] 'Financiación', *Podemos*, https://podemos.info/financiacion/?lang=en; 'Transparencia', *Podemos*, https://transparencia.podemos.info

zipper lists as they present male names followed by female ones in zipper formation – ensuring equal gender representation. The young party workers were given salaries capped at a low €1,900 per month – all surplus cash is channelled into Podemos' activities.[114]

Podemos presented itself as a channel into which the existing anger and political agitation could funnel itself. On its launch, it encouraged the establishment of small, local circles – meetings at which people could organise under the Podemos banner. Online circles also exist, linking people across the country with particular focuses, such as one for people with disabilities. This fit with the grassroots sentiment, without the typical structures of traditional parties. Anyone could set them up, and around 900 were created in the first year.

Their EU manifesto was built from the ideas the circles submitted to an online platform, then voted on by members.[115] Anyone could put themselves forward for candidacy in the upcoming election, even if they were members of a different political party. The online platform could also receive donations quickly. The entire EU campaign brought in funds through crowdfunding, and more to hold a Constituent Assembly.[116]

[114] G. Tremlett, 'The Podemos revolution', *Guardian*, www.theguardian.com/world/2015/mar/31/podemos-revolution-radical-academics-changed-european-politics

[115] G. Tremlett, 'The Podemos revolution', *Guardian*, www.theguardian.com/world/2015/mar/31/podemos-revolution-radical-academics-changed-european-politics

[116] C. Frediani, 'How Tech-Savvy Podemos Became One of Spain's Most Popular Parties in 100 Days', *Techpresident*,

http://techpresident.com/news/wegov/25235/how-tech-savvy-podemos-became-one-spain's-most-popular-parties-100-days

In 2017, nearly half of funding was from grants from the government, but the rest was through donations.[117] The average Spanish electoral campaign costs €2 million, and Podemos matched neither the funding nor the vote share the bigger parties did in 2014. But the crowdsourcing money comes with no strings attached, and perhaps encourages further individual participation.

Balancing Act

High levels of direct democracy might suit a social movement, but Podemos' directors are cautious about its limitations.

The EU manifesto, designed by the circles, included unrealistic promises, such as the introduction of a universal basic income and "non-payment of illegitimate debt."[118] There are also critics who say hierarchical circles of ardent activists and less-avid members have come into existence despite the use of easy-access online organisation. In an interview with *TechPresident*, Simona Levi of *Partido X*, another 15-M political organisation, censured what she terms 'clicktivism', where debates can be won from majority votes with no assurance that those voting are well-informed.[119]

---

[117] 'Transparencia', *Podemos*, https://transparencia.podemos.info

[118] G. Tremlett, 'The Podemos revolution', *Guardian*, www.theguardian.com/world/2015/mar/31/podemos-revolution-radical-academics-changed-european-politics

[119] C. Frediani, 'How Tech-Savvy Podemos Became One of Spain's Most Popular Parties in 100 Days', *Techpresident*,

http://techpresident.com/news/wegov/25235/how-tech-savvy-podemos-became-one-spain's-most-popular-parties-100-days

Loomio is one app which encourages consensus decision-making and has been used by 396 Podemos groups.[120]

Yet, in the main, Podemos' members opted for strong leadership. In another vote that was criticised as ill-informed, Podemos' membership elected one of the organisation's founders, Pablo Iglesias, as Secretary-General.[121] In November 2014, the Constituents' Assembly formally made Podemos into a political organisation – a move that, according to Iglesias himself, created internal systems of control, political and tactical guidelines and organisational efficiency.[122] This make-over, a significant change from 15-M's mass social movement, seems to be considered necessary.

Federico Severino, director of the Podemos foundation, believes you cannot have hybrids – social movements need a political party to win elections and create change. They seem to have softened their ideologies too – Iglesias has made a reference to the organisation's "broad shoulders", the Spanish equivalent of a big tent, which he insists can evolve without loss of enthusiasm. The 2018 budget included relatively moderate pledges to raise the minimum salary and control

---

[120] C. Frediani, 'How Tech-Savvy Podemos Became One of Spain's Most Popular Parties in 100 Days', *Techpresident*,

http://techpresident.com/news/wegov/25235/how-tech-savvy-podemos-became-one-spain's-most-popular-parties-100-days

[121] G. Tremlett, 'The Podemos revolution', *Guardian*, www.theguardian.com/world/2015/mar/31/podemos-revolution-radical-academics-changed-european-politics

[122] P. Iglesias, 'Understanding Podemos', *New Left Review*, 93, https://newleftreview.org/II/93/pablo-iglesias-understanding-podemos

rent levels.[123] The call for abolition of the monarchy has quietened for now.

Under the New Media

This is not simply a softening of radicalism – Podemos' success has come largely from its understanding of the common mood, not its fealty to the impassioned fringes. Consequently, they have demonstrated an impressive ability to speak to the public. Podemos' initial leadership was made-up of academics from Madrid's Complutense University, who, along with student associations, set-up a local neighbourhood television show called *La Tuerka*, which translates as "The Screw". It aimed to provide a space for left-wing debate, whilst being funny and easily watchable.[124]

In his 2015 article to the *New Left Review*, Iglesias cites Italian political scientist Antonio Gramsci's theory of cultural hegemony as the reason for putting resources into media: *"TV studios have become the real parliaments"*, the Secretary-General writes.[125] Not everyone has a degree in political science – but the majority of people enjoy watching television.

With Spain's quasi-tradition of political talk shows, *La Tuerka* fits right in. Thanks to online video-sharing sites, it gained a large following, and has become a focal-point for similar-minded people. It is currently in its fifth season, and

[123] J. Macros, A. Macros, 'Spain's Podemos', *El Pais*, https://elpais.com/elpais/2018/10/16/inenglish/1539692544_763322.html?rel=str_a rticulo#1540831123832

[124] G. Tremlett, 'The Podemos revolution', *Guardian*, www.theguardian.com/world/2015/mar/31/podemos-revolution-radical-academics-changed-european-politics

[125] P. Iglesias, 'Understanding Podemos', *New Left Review*, 93, https://newleftreview.org/II/93/pablo-iglesias-understanding-podemos

Podemos' has expanded its communication channels with the creation of *Público*, a more polished online news site.[126]

Aside from spreading a political message, *La Tuerka* also gave the subsequent Podemos' leadership a de facto doctorate in media wizardry. Severino, who also leads the think-tank 25-M and works to "counter audio-visual disputes", places emphasis on the persuasive tool of entertainment in the modern media landscape. Dry academic debates must be strictly behind-the-scenes. Instead, Podemos engages with the sort of exciting emotional language that draws them the label populist.

Three years after *La Tuerka* began, Iglesias found himself invited onto conservative-leaning current affairs talk shows. He acquitted himself well, perhaps thanks to a televisual presenter's course he had taken, and became a big name in Spanish politics.[127] Political ideas were laid out as common sense, and a response to current crises. Matching the openness of 15-M, which saw the national flag waved alongside the old 1930s Republican one, Iglesias avoided identifying with the old symbols of the left.

To gain ground, Podemos had to appeal to the middle class, too.[128] The targets of Iglesias' critique were the EU Central Bank and other international elites, whom he called *"la casta"* and who had robbed Spain of her sovereignty. These

[126] G. Tremlett, 'The Podemos revolution', *Guardian*, www.theguardian.com/world/2015/mar/31/podemos-revolution-radical-academics-changed-european-politics

[127] G. Tremlett, Giles, 'The Podemos revolution', *Guardian*, www.theguardian.com/world/2015/mar/31/podemos-revolution-radical-academics-changed-european-politics

[128] P. Iglesias, 'Understanding Podemos', *New Left Review*, 93, https://newleftreview.org/II/93/pablo-iglesias-understanding-podemos

uncomplex terms have universal appeal, bolstered by their emotional tone.

This comes back to 15-M and democracy. Podemos *capitalised* on a political climate of distrust shared across the political spectrum. "People do not vote for policies", Severino says, but they support parties that represent their discontent. Podemos, which translates as "We Can!", suggests a move forward and change in the nation's future. The possibility of substantial change can be found in this new political organisation. The direction isn't right or left – "it's about up and down". Severino adds that the main work is being done by the public themselves. Through the media, Podemos delivers talking points which people can debate "in the streets, in the bars".

TV Show and Political Party

Podemos captures the public mood and uses it to present a pathway. It is left-wing and offers left-wing policies – but these policies are always framed as a reasoned and balanced response to contemporary problems.

The 2008 crisis has faded somewhat in 2018, but by *El Pais'* calculations, Podemos may hold the balance of power by 2020.[129] This may be because Podemos adapts to modern politics without losing some conventional strengths: the membership exercises its voice through the circles, but internal structures mean Podemos is still an electoral party rather than a social movement.

Podemos' most impressive trait is its understanding of modern Spanish media. It builds a support base on one

[129] J. Macros, A. Macros, 'Spain's Podemos', *El Pais*,
https://elpais.com/elpais/2018/10/16/inenglish/1539692544_763322.html?rel=str_articulo#1540831123832

channel, whilst avoiding alienating the rest of the population on another channel.

Podemos is a party which *knows* its audience.

Annex
Essays by Domestic Authors

Authors

Magdalena Polan: Senior Fellow at Radix. Formerly, economist at the International Monetary Fund and Senior Economist at Goldman Sachs

Corrado Poli: Founder, Radix Italia and Senior Fellow, Radix UK. Journalist and author writing on social, environmental and political issues

Koen Vossen: Lecturer at Radboud University and author of *The Power of Populism, The Rise of Geert Wilders and the Party for Freedom* (Routledge 2016)

Nicholas J Frizli: Director-General of the World Pensions Council (WPC) and Advisory Board Member of the World Bank Global Infrastructure Facility (GIF)

Antónia Casellas: Associate Professor, Department of Geography, Universitat Autònoma de Barcelona

NOWOCZESNA, POLAND

by Magdalena Polan

'N'owoczesna' stands for 'modern' or 'progressive', and is an antonym to 'old fashioned'.

Nowoczesna was initially promoted as .N, or NowoczesnaPL, to make the name look like an internet domain. The full name of the party used to be 'Nowoczesna of Ryszard Petru' (Ryszard Petru being the founder) but was shortened to 'Nowoczesna' after he stepped down as the leader.

Platform and ideology

Nowoczesna is a liberal, centrist party, both economically and socially.

On the economic front, it argues for economic freedom and support for modern economy based on entrepreneurship and innovation. It argues for an active role of the state through legislation and regulation, but otherwise limited direct engagement in the economy.

For example, the party would like to introduce identical, linear tax rates for individuals, companies, and on consumption (3x16%). It has argued for lower costs of employment and for 'smart' welfare, especially incentives for taking up work or having more children. It supports Poland's entry in the Euro area.

On the legal side, it argues for efficient state and legal system and the classic role of the state and government as providers of supportive legal structure. It has argued strongly for observing the rule of law and supported the independence of the judiciary. It would introduce a two-term limit for parliamentarians and allow voting through the internet.

On the social side, it argues for the separation of church and state (a contentious issue in Poland), equality, openness to migration, as well as accepting the refugees. It supports civic society and civic engagement, and appropriate programs to educate the citizens about their rights and how they could influence politics. It would reform the health system to improve and equalize access. It would also introduce civil unions (including for same-sex couples).

Nowoczesna belongs to the Alliance of Liberals and Democrats for Europe Party (formerly known as the Party of European Liberals, Democrats and Reformers).

Market gap for the new party

Nowoczesna responded to the gap in political representation of socially and economically liberal voters who were disappointed with growing conservatism of then governing party, the Civic Platform (the PO), and the abandonment of more radical or visionary policies.

Aside from those disappointed with the slow pace of progress, the .N captured the frustrations of the entrepreneurial, active, and educated younger Poles who were afraid that the political process was being hijacked by short-term objectives. These people wanted the Polish political system and society to remain progressive and liberal, and the governments to continue with changes that would make the country more similar to Western Europe. Because of this, Nowoczesna also attracted older voters who were both proud of Poland's progress but also disappointed with the slowing pace of economic and social reforms.

But the party also responded to the needs of the classically liberal voters. These people wanted to see the government more as an enabler of an efficient state, leaving people to take care of their businesses and communities. In this way, they attracted those who valued the civil society and recognized its importance in local and national policies and political representation, as well as entrepreneurs.

In this context, Nowoczesna stood out from many new European parties as being a pro-reform party of the middle- and upper-class, and not a populist party. And it arose mostly from hunger for more ambitious change, and not as a direct response to a crisis (since Poland was not heavily affected by the 2008 and Eurozone crises).

Nowoczesna also attracted quite some women. They were attracted by the progressive agenda rejecting more radical leftist solutions and a high share of women in party leadership.

The victory of Law and Justice (the PiS) candidate Andrzej Duda in May 2015 presidential elections and the disappointment with presidential campaigns of the other candidates strengthened the appetite for a more modern, active, and hungry political party.

Formation

Nowoczesna was formed by Ryszard Petru, and officially established in May 2015, ahead of October 2015 parliamentary elections. Petru was already known to the public as an economist and a pundit; he also had experience in the business sector. At the time of its founding, the party was called 'Nowoczesna of Ryszard Petru', elevating the profile of the founder. But the name got shortened to 'Nowoczesna' after Petru stepped down as a leader in November 2017.

The other key founders came from among local councillors of various larger and medium-sized cities, local activists, entrepreneurs, lawyers, and economists. This way, the new party tapped into the wide, national pool of people experienced at local politics or activism, and having business experience.

Cities outside Warsaw have always been important to Polish politics. Economic and cultural activity in Poland is spread across multiple centers, even though Warsaw remains the key political and business hub. But the industry, many family-owned companies, and a few important business sectors like shipping, mining, or car production are located outside Warsaw. These cities also have well-regarded universities, so can benefit from having their own intellectual and business elites.

They also have experienced local leaders. Many Polish and other Central European cities and villages suffered from post-communist, post-industrial decline and had to reinvent themselves, against limited welfare assistance and transfers from the central government. Competition for investments, jobs, and later the EU funds, produced a large number of people who were skilled, active, experienced, and had appetite for larger things.

Most of the members were political newbies. 85% of Nowoczesna members had not belonged to a political party before. All of the 28 Nowoczesna MPs who entered the parliament in 2015 were first-time MPs.

Campaign, mobilization, and the media

Nowoczesna had a fairly standard campaign in the traditional media. Party activists did well on TV and stood up well against more familiar politicians from the major parties. But they were not only fresh faces. They were polite but assertive in their appearances. Various Nowoczesna representatives frequented the media, helping attract women and people who wanted to support someone from their town or region.

As most of the modern parties, they used the internet extensively. They made frequent use of visual ads, often collages of pictures, slogans, and own commentary, designed to be understood quickly, and usually published after relevant events or statements from other parties. These internet adds most of the time referred back to the Nowoczesna's program to explain how the party proposed to deal with the issue in question, or how the issue would not have arose if they were in power. This helped the party deliver the message repeatedly, and brought attention to their program using real life examples. They also had snappy – but always civilized – tweets. They continued this strategy after the elections.

After the elections and a change of leadership

Nowoczesna received 7.6% of votes in 2015 elections. Afterwards, its support has fluctuated from barely 5% (so just about clearing the entry threshold) to 20%, for some time surpassing that of the PO, the main opposition party.

Their popularity took a hit in late 2016. In December 2016, opposition parties were occupying the speaker's stand in the Parliament to block a draft law that they deemed unconstitutional. But as the blockade was under way, Petru was photographed on a holiday flight with a female colleague. The lack of a clear response from the party, as well as the absence of the leader during a challenging moment for the opposition did not go well with the voters.

Disagreements over how to work with the other opposition parties, as well as the cost of Petru's absence during the blockade, led to an eventual change in party leadership. In November 2017, Katarzyna Lubnauer became the chair; the top leadership of the party was also revamped.

Petru subsequently left the party and, together with a few of his Nowoczesna colleagues, created a new movement called Now, with a program close to the original one of Nowoczesna. More members and MPs left after Nowoczesna formed an election bloc with the PO and other opposition parties, owing to the concerns that the much larger PO would eventually dominate Nowoczesna.

Interaction with other parties

Ahead of the 2015 elections, Nowoczesna was a natural competitor to the PO (the Civic Platform), given the PO's liberal origins. But the two did not fight aggressively in the campaign. Still, Nowoczesna was seen as the 'new PO' to some extent. The party did not engage much with the left parties either, but rather tried to present its own realistic solutions to some key issues on the lefts' agenda.

As an opposition party, Nowoczesna initially maintained an uneasy alliance with the PO so as to not to alienate the centrist voters. But both parties – and most of the other opposition parties – took part in rallies against the changes promoted by the PiS-led government.

Eventually, in January 2018, Nowoczesna, the PO, and other parties, agreed to run together in November 2018 local elections. Nowoczesna was relatively successful in these elections. Its own candidates, or those supported by the electoral bloc, won numerous mayoral positions. The electoral bloc also won majorities in just under a half of regional assemblies. Nowoczesna also plans to run together with other opposition parties in 2019 European elections.

Things looked different when it came to the right side of the political spectrum. Before 2015 general elections, Nowoczesna campaigned strongly against the Law and Justice (the PiS) given significant differences in views. And Nowoczesna MPs have proven themselves to be very diligent in the critique of the subsequent Law and Justice government. They have remained focused on referring back to their agenda (like in the campaign) and remained proactive in proposing solutions. They also remained engaged with the civic society organizations but their entry into the parliament and strong focus on active opposition work took them somewhat away from their core agenda.

The party lost some impetus after the departures of Petru and his close colleagues. But the upcoming European and general elections in 2019 are likely to energize the party again. Still, the disillusionment of some members and the fear that Nowoczesna might be completely absorbed by the PO might eat into the energy and enthusiasm that went into 2015 campaign. Nevertheless, Nowoczesna still has a shot at entering the parliament again, unlike most new (smaller) parties before it.

II

Dreaming a radical new politics: The Italian Five Stars Movement[130]

by Corrado Poli

T he word "party" apparently derives from "part". It means that parties represent sections of society. Typically, in the mass society, the classic division was between working class and the bourgeoisie. Later, in some countries like France, Germany and Italy, it transformed into conservative and progressive which shuffled the traditional social class allegiance. In fact, a significant share of the intellectual bourgeoisie joined the working class in their fight to implement more advanced and modern individual rights and social justice in order to accelerate social change.

Thus, after World War II, the crucial political conflict happened between the progressives – supported by and supporting the working class – who wanted to speed up the untamable modernisation, urbanisation, industrialisation and secularisation processes, and the conservatives who tried to slow it down. In some countries, different political features appeared: in Italy and Germany the Christian Democrats were inspired by the idea of class co-operation rather than conflict (Marxists) or just competition (radical libertarians); in the UK and in Italy smaller parties – the Liberals and the Socialists

[130] Note: this article was written before the Five Stars Movement electoral success and their entry into coalition government with La Lega

respectively – formed and played a progressive role by representing a more defined social section.

However, all the political competition happened in a mass society in which life-styles were directly related to social class cultures and later just to income levels, when modernisation was definitely achieved.

This political structure has effectively operated until approximately twenty or so years ago, then it began to decline. Recent social studies claim that we passed from a mass and class society to a new social environment in which people aggregate according to different life-styles or sub-cultures. One might accept or question this approach, consider it temporary or a long-lasting feature of future social organization: however, in the short run, politics is dealing with this unconventional form of social grouping and its contradictory – according to the still reigning nineteenth century philosophies – political choices.

However, political organization is still profoundly rooted in the power and governance system, not to speak of the political rhetoric that still employs outdated unappealing language. Long-established and well-organized traditional parties have occupied the power strongholds. Depending on each country's laws and practices, they are still able to finance themselves and their political campaigns either by public finance or thanks to private donors. And of course, by illegal means and hidden funds. Recently, two major facts have happened that have changed the rules of the political game. First, old parties have gradually lost control of a society that has transformed so that they keep losing more and more fragments of their constituencies. Second, the power-friendly mainstream media are no longer as persuasive as they used to be over the public opinion and are challenged by the social networks that have become the main source of information to most citizens. Political campaigning and the forming of public opinion on the Internet is way cheaper than in newspapers, on TV, door to door and through advertising devices. This major change in the forming of public opinion has reduced the competitiveness of the conventional political organisations that are not practically and philosophically fit to cope in the new informational environment. Incidentally, this radical change only partly regards the individual social values which tend to be quite stable; essentially it concerns the governance and representation system. Though the vote-shifts have increased significantly in recent years, voters' loyalty to "their own" party is usually hard to undermine.

The Five Stars movement typically refuses funds that the government appropriates to parties for their political campaigns. Because they cannot refuse the money, they created a fund to support new companies and build infrastructure (which admittedly is another form of propaganda). Also, the Members of Parliament devolve a large part of their allowances for the same purposes. However, to start the successful Grillo's blog and in general to make the movement move the first steps, some substantial investment was likely necessary. This money probably came from the Casaleggio company and other investors. Everyday political activity is completely self-financed by activists.

In some respect, Italy has been the harbinger of the ongoing radical political change. Berlusconi's style has anticipated Trump in large Western countries, though this is not something to be proud of. More recently, that is in the last ten years, and more intensively in the last five, the Five Stars movement (they refuse to be called a "party") has been challenging the party system establishment. They began as a protest populist faction led by Beppe Grillo, a brilliant comedian who transformed political rallies into real shows. But Grillo has never been an alien to politics: since the eighties his shows were highly politicised to the extent that he was banned from Italian public television networks for his repeated challenge to the ruling classes.

Differently from other political movements, since the beginning they used internet and social networks. Thanks to a smart communication strategy developed by Gian Roberto Casaleggio, Grillo's mentor, his blog soon became one of the most visited in the world.

Five Stars' voters are quite diverse among them in many respects; they are united by mainly expressing a plain protest vote triggered by a generic discontent generated by the economic and social crisis. On the other hand, the movement's activists are younger and more educated than in other parties' organisations for two major reasons: (a) the crucial role of the Internet and virtual contacts; (b) besides the protest against the government that collected the most emotional vote, the movement's messages focused on issues such as environment and connectivity. As a consequence, women are more active than in other political formations independently from equal opportunity laws.

Because of this particular membership, Five Stars movement's platform and basic values are considerably different from other populist parties who are successful all over Europe and the United States – if you consider Trump part of them. Mainly, the movement does not represent the right sector and is free from any fascist or Nazi legacy, neither does it call for the preservation of old traditions or some national identity. Activists are future-oriented, non-violent and anti-war, socially inclusive with immigrants, pro-education, etc. And straightforwardly against the establishment!

If they refuse some typical European right sector slogans, does it mean they are leftists? They are not in as much as they are not rightists. They fish in both constituencies and mainly among the people who would not vote if the Five Stars were not there. In other words, they aim at representing the unrepresented who, to a large extent, are the educated new "prof-letarians": young professional Europeans, with no children and no (or unsatisfactory) jobs.

Prof-letarians have a high opinion of themselves and this is good (why not?). The problem is that they also have unachievable high expectations about income and social status. These thirtyish-fortyish people are unlikely to gain the income and the social status they aim at because currently the supply of educated people is abundant compared to the demand. Therefore, they are frustrated and see in the Five Stars both an opportunity for a new policy and a way to express their anger against a society that in their opinion marginalises them. They are teachers (who would like to be) academicians, professional trained in not yet well-established careers, lawyers, musicians, artists, and in general people active and skilled in jobs that still lack a competitive market.

Surprisingly, these still generic ideological features of the participants in the movement, have not been explicitly elaborated either by some self-proclaimed or elected leader nor do they refer to some intellectual elaboration. At least, this is the common perception at first glance. Critics of the movement claim that there was a hidden strategy in diffusing short repetitive and apparently occasional messages that in the long term created and are creating the shared ideology or language of the movement.

The movements' promoters reply that Five Stars' ideology is merely the outcome of the way the activists aggregate on the net. They maintain that the political proposals of the movement emerge from an open debate and are voted online. Thus, citizens first aggregate online, then ideas, a proposal and eventually the overall platform follow. In a way, it proves the famous McLuhan's quote "the medium is the message". In this respect, the movement is ideology-free, but at the same time it represents a part of the electorate that lacks or distrusts membership in other parties.

Adversaries of the movement have been and still are suspicious of the role of the *Casaleggio Associati*, a well-established public relations and communication company somehow connected with financial power. The company was led, until his premature death last year, by Gian Roberto Casaleggio a media and communication expert and a visionary. Someone suspected that the grassroots (or internet) democracy endorsed by the movement was indeed heavily conditioned by the *Casaleggio Associati*. Certainly, Gian Roberto Casaleggio who bequeathed the company direction to his son Davide, played a major role in the establishment of the movement. Whether the *Casaleggio Associati* responds to some real "stay-behind" power is uncertain and definitely unproven.

It is also difficult to foretell whether the *Casaleggio Associati* or some external interest group can really keep under control the online voting system and the very flexible structure of the movement. They might have created an organisation purposely designed to go out of their control. Nonetheless, and contrary to traditional politics, this is an irrelevant issue.

As a matter of fact, the movement's leaders are not interested in implementing their own ideas and convincing the electorate to follow them. Rather they want to find and lead an electorate that forms online as the output of a poll. The founders of Five Stars' politics believe that their role is not to propose ideas and programs, but to represent what the people communicate. Political philosophers would argue a lot about the pros and cons of this approach, but it is definitely a new entry that cannot be included into the long-lasting dualism between right versus left, labour versus conservative, socialism versus libertarianism.

Moreover, differently from the traditional politics, the Five Star constituencies form on the net and have no direct contact either with geography or with established institutions like unions, clubs, associations, vested interests, churches and so on. The movement's elected members call themselves "citizens' voice" (*portavoce* in Italian) and they don't like the word "leader" given to the most prominent persons that obviously arose in the course of time.

There is a clear conceptual contradiction: an ideology that refuses ideology is a strong ideology especially because it is foreign to any well-established political and scholarly tradition. Thus, to promote it you need convincing leaders and to achieve political success an elaborated organisation – no matter if just virtual – is required. A scholarly and in-depth analysis of this aspect is still to be elaborated.

In the beginning, the Five Stars' representatives refused to participate in any TV political talk-show and didn't release interviews to newspapers because they did not trust mainstream media independence. This was also a communication strategy that worked well to create an aura of diversity and curiosity. After having elected several members of Parliament and other representative in civil institutions, the movement's leaders dismissed the ban and now the participation is equal to other political groups. Five Stars' communication style has not influenced significantly other parties. But they have been somewhat effective in fighting against corruption and in forcing the government to pass some laws they proposed or sustained. For instance, if the Five Stars were not loudly calling for a reduction of politicians' privileges, it would have been unlikely that the Parliament would reduce their members' allowances.

One major characteristic of Five Stars is that they refuse to participate in any coalition with other parties both at state level and locally. This has become particularly inconvenient because the new electoral law – clearly designed to penalise the movement which in the polls is supposed to be the first party – favours party coalitions by assigning the majority in the Parliament to the coalition (and not to the single party) that wins more votes than the others. The refusal to make any alliance is meant to stress the diversity of the movement from any other political group. It's possible – if not likely – that, after the election, especially if the votes of the Five Stars will be necessary to form a government, the movement will split in two parts: the fundamentalists and the collaborationists.

The movement lacks any grassroots organisation, hence it performs poorly in local elections in which often it is not even interested to participate actively. Their aggregation is not physical and they can perform well in large metropolises – that by the way are not so numerous in Italy whose population mostly lives in small towns – and at national or European level.

The future of the Five Stars movement is uncertain. They have been an active and influential opposition for almost five years now. The turning point will be the next Parliamentary elections that will take place next spring in Italy. Some analysts think that it might dissolve as quickly as it was established because of its very light and virtual structure. Others believe that it will last and other parties are indeed imitating the same strategy and party organisation. Whatever happens in real politics, one thing is certain: Casaleggio and the Five Stars brought into politics lots of new ideas with which everyone will have to deal with in the future.

III

A One-Man Orchestra in the Netherlands: Geert Wilders and the Party for Freedom (PVV)[131]

by Koen Vossen

For a long period of time, the most famous Dutch were painters, soccer-players and members of the royal family. The names of Dutch politicians used to be rather unknown as politics in the Netherlands seldom attracted attention of the outside world.

But, since the turn of the century, things seem to have changed. A few Dutch politicians have acquired some fame outside the Netherlands, such as Pim Fortuyn, the political maverick who was assassinated in 2002, Ayaan Hirsi Ali, a liberal Member of Parliament who became one of the most eloquent critics of Islam in Europe and finally Geert Wilders, at the moment probably the most well-known Dutch politician.

Wilders's fame is based on his remarkable ability to find the national and international spotlights with radical statements and sensational actions as well as on the

---

[131] The direct quotes in this article come from: Koen Vossen, Rondom Wilders. Portret van de PVV (Amsterdam 2013)

spectacular rise of his party, the Partij voor de Vrijheid (Party for Freedom; PVV).

In 2006, the PVV made a relatively modest first appearance in the national elections (5.9% of the votes), after which the party peaked at the European elections in 2009 (17%) and the national elections in 2010 (15.5%). After these last elections, a minority coalition of Liberals and Christian Democrats was formed, which was tolerated by the PVV in exchange for influence on the governmental policy, especially on immigration and asylum policy.

This minority government stayed in power for 18 months, after which Wilders decided to withdraw his support in protest at austerity measures being imposed on the Netherlands by the European Union. In electoral terms, this proved to be a misjudgement as his party lost one-third of its electorate in the 2012 national elections.

Moreover, his abrupt move has put his party back in isolation, distrusted by fairly all relevant political parties in the Netherlands. Still, however, the PVV seems to be on their way back, at least in the polls, which show a rather constant increase.

The founding of the PVV

The PVV was officially founded in February 2006, but its date of birth could also be placed somewhat earlier.

In September 2004, Geert Wilders left the VVD, the conservative-liberal party which had been his political home since 1990. Between 1990 and 1998 Wilders had been an assistant for the parliamentary group of the VVD, at that moment the third party of the Netherlands. In 1998, Wilders became a Member of Parliament. He soon earned a reputation as a fierce critic of the Dutch welfare state and the consultation system in socio-economic affairs, but also as one of the first politicians who warned for the danger of Islamic terrorism and weapons of mass destruction in the Middle East.

Since his first visit to Israel and some of its Arab neighbours in 1981, Wilders was fascinated by the conflict in the Middle East. After 9/11, 2001 Wilders became an unjustly ignored whistle-blower, who was often invited onto talk shows to talk on Islam. Though Wilders was a fierce supporter of the American War on Terror and all accessory measures, his opinion on Islam was still rather moderate. He distanced himself openly from Pim Fortuyn, a former professor of sociology who, in the autumn of 2001, attracted a lot of publicity with his fierce criticism of the Dutch immigration policy and what he called the 'Islamisation of our culture'.

By attacking Islam because of its alleged 'backwardness', Fortuyn seemed to have found an essential ingredient which made it possible to be progressive and to criticise immigration and the multicultural society at the same time.

Nine days after Fortuyn was assassinated by an animal rights activist on the 6 May 2002, his party attained 17 per cent of the vote and became the second-largest party in parliament. Especially, the VVD had lost a lot of votes to the LPF. As a result, Wilders was forced to leave parliament which, according to many accounts, must have been a traumatic experience for the passionate parliamentarian that Wilders had become.

When Wilders came back as a Member of Parliament, he began to present himself more and more as Fortuyn's heir. He advocated all kinds of radical measures against those who (could) threaten Dutch security, which were inspired by American and Israeli examples (for example, declaring a state of emergency, preventive arrests, administrative detentions and the possible denaturalisation).

In the beginning, Wilders considered such measures only suitable for real terrorists, but gradually he also included radical imams and even Moroccan criminals. Finally, Wilders began criticizing Islam as a whole and, together with Ayaan Hirsi Ali, his fellow liberal MP, he called for a 'liberal jihad' against the advancing threat of political Islam.

In the summer of 2004, Wilders' position within the VVD became untenable and on 1 September 2004, he left the parliamentary club but – due to the Dutch electoral law – he was able to hold on to his seat in parliament.

The ideology of the PVV

Initially, Wilders made plans to establish a neo-conservative party in the Netherlands. For that reason, he had made contact with Bart Jan Spruyt, chairman of the Edmund Burke Foundation, a relatively new think tank which was devoted to spreading conservative ideology in a country that perceived itself as eminently progressive.

Relying on the polls, the neo-conservative programme did not strike a chord and, in the summer of 2006, Wilders changed the course of the party. Together with Martin Bosma, a former journalist and an expert in (and fan of) American campaigning-strategies, Wilders succeeded in shaping a distinct political programme and strategy which proved to be highly successful.

The PVV-ideology is based on *four pillars*: islam-alarmism, nationalism, populism and law and order. Almost all the viewpoints of the PVV are related to one of these pillars.

For Wilders and Bosma, the first pillar, islam-alarmism, is probably the most important one. Islam-alarmism is based on an essentialist vision of Islam as a totalitarian ideology which is in time and space absolute and invariable. Islam is from its early beginnings aiming to conquer the whole world and the submission of all other religions. After previous attempts to conquer Europe (in 732 and 1683) proved a failure, Islam has developed a new strategy for the Islamification of Europe, that is immigration and intimidation.

Various examples are perceived as evidence of this theory: terrorist attacks, Moroccan youth gangs, high number of unemployed Muslims, increased homophobia and anti-semitism due to Muslims. But also those Muslims who seem to have integrated into Dutch society are, according to the PVV, suspect. According to the Islamic dogma *Taqqia*, Muslims living in non-Muslim-counties have the right to hide their true beliefs, Wilders stated.

Whereas he initially demanded strict assimilation, he now called for an almost complete marginalisation of Muslims, who relying on the Taqqia-doctrine are by definition untrustworthy. Examples of this are his pleas for banning the Koran and closing all mosques and his proposal for a tax for headscarves, which he called a 'headrag-tax'.

This fierce opposition to Islam is accompanied by an even stronger dislike of the elite. Wilders copied Fortuyn's rhetoric against an alleged monopoly of Dutch politics and public opinion by a 'church of the left wing', a homogeneous and self-serving progressive caste, who refused to acknowledge the threat of Islam to the liberal and libertarian Dutch values.

Following Bat Ye'or's infamous Eurabia theory, Wilders has claimed that the immigration of Muslims was permitted by left-wing political parties, who hoped to gain a new, loyal constituency after the loss of their old constituency.

From 2006 onwards, Wilders referred more often to this old constituency of the left-wing political parties, the 'common people', Henk and Ingrid, who are fed up with criminality, Islamisation, and politics in general and who demand immediate deeds. To make their voice louder, Wilders advocates a more direct democracy with referenda and direct elections of mayors, police commissioner and even judges. *'Not the political elite, but the people should have the opportunity to express more often their will, because together the people know better as that left-wing clique'*, the 2010 party programme reads.

The third pillar is a strong nationalism, that has more emphasis on the national interests and national values and an increasing dislike for supranational co-operation.

Already in 2005, Wilders launched a successful no-campaign in the referendum on the proposed EU-treaty. From 2010 on, Wilders began to plea for a full Dutch exit out of the European Union and the Euro. The resistance to the EU was especially based on the imposed solidarity with Greece and other southern countries, but perhaps even more on the EU-regulations on immigration and asylum-policy, which made it difficult for the Netherlands to implement a strict immigration policy.

In the 2012 national election-campaign, the PVV focused on its opposition to the 'Superstate' European Union with the slogan *'Less Brussels, more Netherlands'*. Switzerland and Norway now served as example of countries which were still masters of their own destiny. Other signs of an increasing nationalism were pleas for promoting national pride on schools (flag ceremonies, national history) and a rather optional proposal to integrate the Flemish part of Belgium into the Dutch nation.

Also, the nationalist program has a strong nativist and welfare-chauvinistic dimension. *´Our hard-earned welfare state is a source of pride, but in the last decades it has become a magnet for lower educated immigrants,'* maintains the PVV in its 2010 election programme.

The PVV opposed the facilitation of laws relating to dismissal, the increase of the retirement age and cuts to the minimum wage, while advocating more investment in healthcare and facilities for the elderly. The access to the welfare state should however be restricted to the Dutch and to immigrants who have worked and lived in the Netherlands for at least ten years and have assimilated (that is those who are able to speak Dutch, don't wear a burqa and have no criminal record).

To be sure, Wilders also stuck to more harsh economic measures such as a cut down on expenses on development aid, culture and arts, public broadcasting service, environmental policy and the asylum and immigration policy.

Last but not least, Wilders and Bosma had worked out an extensive 'law and order' paragraph. Their measures appear to be inspired by robust American policies on crime, such as those by New York's mayor Rudolf Giuliani ('zero tolerance, three strikes, you're out') and Arizona-sheriff Joe Arpaio ('pink dressed criminals in a public chain-gang').

At the same time, the PVV opposes the death penalty and the right to bear arms and also is, especially from an American perspective, quite libertarian with regard to the right for abortion, embryo selection, euthanasia and gay-marriage. The party even offered a resolution in parliament to allow gay soldiers to wear their military outfit in the gay-parade.

This more libertarian aspect of the PVV-programme has puzzled many observers in the Netherlands and abroad. How can a party that in most respects is almost a copy of nationalist-populist parties such as Front National, Vlaams Belang, Freiheitliche Partei Österreichs or Lega Nord be such a fierce defender of women and gay emancipation? The answer is that Wilders in this respect has followed Fortuyn who, as mentioned, combined progressive, libertarian viewpoints with criticism of Islam, which was perceived as a threat to Dutch modernity.

However, Wilders certainly has gone a few steps further than the more liberal-populist Fortuyn, as demonstrated by his proposals to ban the Koran, to close all mosques, to introduce a 'head-rag tax' and to restrict the welfare state to assimilated Dutch citizens. In this process of radicalization, Wilders eventually ended up in the nationalist-populist party family which he initially tried to avoid.

In a sense, Wilders acknowledged this by eventually seeking contact with Marine Le Pen and the leaders of the

Lega Nord and Vlaams Belang in 2013. The main goal of their rapprochement – to form a parliamentary group in the European Parliament – eventually failed, but their alliance indicates that the PVV perceives itself now more and more as part of the European family of nationalist-populist parties.

Looking at Wilders' political career, one may see a clear radicalisation. From a conservative-liberal opponent of the welfare state, Wilders has developed into one of the most prominent nationalist-populist politicians in Europe. The question of course is what can explain this development? Is Wilders just a smart political entrepreneur looking for votes?

Probably. Wilders and Bosma, both political professionals, were well aware that there were many votes to be gained with a program that combined welfare chauvinism, euro-scepticism, law and order and anti-immigration.

Still, sheer opportunism does not explain everything. The radical Islam-alarmism is, in electoral terms, probably not very appealing and has, moreover, damaged the coalition potential of the party. This aspect is for Wilders, however, of crucial importance, as he has often repeated. It thus seems to be unsatisfactory to just perceive Wilders as an opportunistic demagogue, for whom only the polls count.

Two other aspects should be taken into account. First of all, Wilders is already, for more than ten years, living at a secret address and under 24-hour police protection. This means that almost every step Wilders takes, and also in his private life, has to be planned because of the need for security measures. His name ranks high on an Al Qaeda death list, on which Salman Rushdie, Charlie Hebdo's Stéphane Charbonnier and the Danish cartoonist Kurt Westergaard are included. The events in Paris in January 2015 have shown that these threats have to be taken very seriously.

Of course, it is difficult to prove that these constant death threats and the difficult living conditions that Wilders is facing, have caused the evident process of political radicalisation he has gone through since 2005-2006. Still, one does not have to be a professional psychologist to suspect that the permanent presence of bodyguards has done little to put his belief in the advancing threat of Islam into some perspective.

A second aspect which may explain this process of radicalising is the choice for a party model without official members (besides Wilders himself).

The relatively liberal legislation regarding party organisation enables Wilders to hang on to this unusual party model, although by doing so he misses out a substantial sum of public funding which in the Netherlands is only granted to parties with more than a thousand members. So the party's MPs and representatives in the provincial and local councils, as well as all the party activists, are technically not members of the PVV, but mere employees or volunteers, without official means to have a say in internal matters.

The result of this unique party model is, first of all, that the PVV is a relatively poor party. The election campaigns are, compared to those of most other parties, very modest and amateurish. In part, the PVV resorts to other, cheaper means of communication such as social media and various websites. The most important channel of communication, however, is by means of the traditional media, the newspapers, magazines, television and radio-networks.

Lacking the money to direct their own publicity campaign, the PVV almost completely relies on free publicity, which Wilders generates by his frequent provocative statements and actions. The permanent need for media attention is therefore at the centre of most political activities of the PVV. So, in parliament, Wilders and his fellow-MPs made particular use of their oversight authority while avoiding the less mediagenic and time-consuming legislative procedures.

The PVV therefore submitted a whole series of written and oral questions, resolutions and often called for emergency debates and interpellations. Most resolutions did not stand a chance and were above all meant to provoke. Moreover, the PVV used a language which was quite unusual in the serene and conciliatory parliamentary culture of the Netherlands.

The PVV accused the government of straightforward lies and deceit and ministers of being *'raving mad'*, having a *'spine of whipped cream'* whereas, young Moroccan criminals were continuously referred to as *'street terrorists'* or *'Muslim-colonists'*, political themes such as environment, culture and development aid were *'left-wing hobbies'* and politicians who were too soft on Islam were named *'politically correct cowards'*.

In parliament, but also in the public debate on television and in newspapers, the language and the actions of the PVV resulted in fierce reactions and debates. The main beneficiary of these debates was of course the PVV, who managed to dominate Dutch media for another week. Yet, to continue attracting the attention of the media, ever more radical statements have to be made, and more spectacular events have to be organized. It is only via the media that Wilders' constituency receives any knowledge on the activities of the party.

In other words, the memberless party-model has made the party to a large extent dependent on free publicity, which is again an incentive for radicalising. In that sense the PVV may be best perceived as a one-man band which is playing louder and louder to attract our attention.

It remains an open question exactly how loud Wilders will play in the future.

References

-Art, D.& S.L. de Lange, Fortuyn versus Wilders. An Agency-Based Approach to Radical Right Party Building.' *West European Politics* 34, no. 6 (2011)

-Bosma, M., *De schijnélite van de valse munters. Drees, extreem rechts, de sixties, nuttige idioten, Groep Wilders en ik.* (Amsterdam 2010)

-Lucardie, P. & G. Voerman, 'Geert Wilders and the Party for Freedom in the Netherlands: A Political Entrepreneur in the Polder', Karsten Grabow & Florian Hartleb, *Exposing the Demagogues. Right-Wing and National-Populist Parties in Europe.* (Berlin 2013)

-Mudde, C., *Populist radical-right parties in Europe* (Cambridge 2007)

-Vossen, K. *Rondom Wilders. Portret van de PVV* (Amsterdam 2013)

-Wilders, G., *Kies voor vrijheid. Een eerlijk antwoord* (z.pl. 2005)

-Wilders, G., *Marked for death .Islam's War against the West and Me* (New York 2012)

-Wilders, G., *Marked for death .Islam's War against the West and Me* (New York 2012)

III

La République En Marche: Macron's Resolute Walk Towards Radical Centrism[132]

by M. Nicolas J. Firzli

The year 2017 saw the unravelling of the prevailing order that had dominated the French political scene since the late 1950s (end of the Fourth Republic).

For nearly sixty years (1958-2017), the authoritarian centre-right Gaullists shared France's *'fromage'* (cushy public jobs, neoclassical Left Bank mansions and lightly-clad assistants) with the moderately Marxist Socialists. Apart from a short hiatus (the 1976-80 Raymond Barre government), that period was marked by the progressive decline and eventual marginalisation of the eminently French *Radicale* tradition – once Western Europe's leading political philosophy.

It took Emmanuel Macron less than a year to revive it by using a bold combination of modern managerial techniques, digital marketing and age-old tactical manoeuvrings: to this day, France's Labour party ('Socialists'), Gaullist Conservatives ('LR') and right-wing nationalists ('FN') don't seem to know what hit them.

---

[132] This article was written before recent political events notably the *gilets jaune* protests

A Young Man in a Hurry

Emmanuel Macron's life seems to mirror that of Pierre Nioxe, the workaholic character from a famous mid-century Parisian novel *"who suffers from a curious affliction: he insists on doing everything quickly."*[133]

A former Jacobin statist (of the Chevènement genre) turned laissez-faire investment banker, Macron failed to secure a nomination to run as Socialist Party candidate in the Amiens district (2007) and eventually joined the office of president Hollande in 2012 as economic advisor and deputy-director, a rather derivative role. For two years, the "economic policy memos" Macron churned out were systematically discarded by a wimpish president. Macron chafed under the old orthodoxies of French social-democracy, but eventually rose through the ranks and became Minister of the Economy in 2014, a position in which he served for just two years.

Unable to push through the overdue employment law reforms (the *'Code du Travail'* was to a large extent the brainchild of Cold War Era Communist-leaning legislators), Macron eventually resigned in the summer of 2016. Back then, most political experts believed he was committing political suicide *en direct*.[134]

But his resignation was only the natural consequence of the establishment of En Marche! (known as 'EM'), a new, seemingly modest political movement founded four months earlier (April 2016) by Emmanuel Macron, Benjamin Griveaux, Cédric O, Stanislas Guerini and Ismaël Emelien. Tellingly, four out of five co-founders, including Macron himself, were alumni of the HEC Paris School of Management, France's leading business school founded in 1871 by market-

---

[133] *Review of "The Man in a Hurry."* Publishers Weekly, July 27, 2015

[134] Alemagna, Lilian. "Pourquoi Macron rompt." Libération, 30 August 2016

friendly *Radicaux modérés* and their secular centrist allies (dubbed *"opportunistes"* by their enemies).

The Rebirth of *Belle Époque* Economism

The HEC School of Management was founded precisely at the start of the 'Belle Époque' (late Victorian and Edwardian eras in the UK), a period rightly described as a golden era for a new kind of French culture and civilisation.

The country had been humiliated by the United States (Mexico 1866) and defeated by Germany (Sedan 1870), and the new French elites (*"les nouvelles couches sociales"*) sought to transform their country as rapidly as possible into a modern nation which could compete with Washington and Berlin on the world stage. To that end, they pursued a dual policy combining ambitious, market-driven economic growth ("centre-right") and anti-clerical secularism across schools, universities and the civil service ("centre-left"), thus breaking away with Catholic-inspired agrarianism, which moderate Radicals and centrists perceived as a hindrance to modernisation (many of them were Anglophile Deists and Lockean *libres-penseurs*, which further fuelled their anticlerical outlook).

Just like Macron and his En Marche friends, the *Radicaux modérés* were obsessed with the comparison with Germany. Guided by "modern, scientific skills", the new managerial class leading French banks, industrial plants, business schools and university research labs were to contribute to the "national effort" – even Dr Louis Pasteur's remarkable discoveries (vaccination, modern microbiology, treatment of tropical diseases) came from the French pharmaceutical sector's urge to beat their Prussian rivals! That resolutely modernist *Radicale-technocratique* worldview, which regards economics as the main factor in society, lost much of its political clout after World War I, as doctrinaire Socialist and Communist collectivism (on the left) and Catholic conservatism, Gaullism and ultra-nationalism (on the right) left very little political space for that once dominant ideology (except perhaps during the short-lived Giscard- Barre era, 1976-80).

François Mitterrand's Socialist Party came to power in 1981 in alliance with the Stalinist left (French Communists being the only unreconstructed Marxists left west of the Iron Curtain) and, paradoxically, with the implicit support of some Gaullist-conservative and right-wing MPs, who despised free-market economics and technocratic modernisation equally – de Gaulle himself had quipped "French politics won't be settled at the Paris Stock Exchange" (*'la politique de la France ne se fait pas à la Corbeille'*). Quite predictably, the period which ensued (1981-2017) was a disaster for the French economy. For nearly four decades, doctrinaire Socialist Party politicians and clumsy provincialist conservatives were to alternate in office, while the French economy sank and the far-right National Front and their Islamist frenemies spread the gospel of ethno-cultural hatred across the country.

Big Tent Centrism and the New New

Many early En Marche backers came from the French private equity and venture capital (PE & VC) industry, a relatively small social set positioned precisely at the crossroads where finance and high-tech meet.

Not surprisingly, most French VC firms are led by alumni of HEC and INSEAD, many of them personal friends and former colleagues of Emmanuel Macron: ambitious entrepreneurs particularly enthusiastic about notions such as "hyper-growth" and "digital leapfrogging".

Conservative and Socialist politicians made no particular effort to reach out to them, while *"at least one candidate competing in the [French] presidential election [was] well-disposed towards the technology sector. Emmanuel Macron championed digital growth when he was economy minister;*

this week [Feb. 23rd 2017] in London he urged French expats to come home to innovate."[135]

Macron's shrewd cultural wink to the 'New-New-Thing' crowd[136] came in the form of a derogatory term he used to describe his rivals, be they mildly Marxist Social-Democrats or rigid Conservatives: *"L'Ancien Monde"* made of fossilised political dinosaurs harking back to the pre-digital age. Tech-sector billionaires (who own many of the country's newspapers, magazines and TV networks) reciprocated by lending their support to the young consigliere's unorthodox campaign. Once a handicap, Macron's youthful demeanour suddenly became an asset in the eyes of France's famously gerontocratic chattering classes.

But En Marche's venture-capitalist vision went far beyond top-down support from generous IT and telecom nouveaux-riches. The new party itself was consciously and conspicuously modelled after Silicon Valley startups: *"Key to Macron's success is the army of volunteers – known by the English term 'helpers' – who give up their time to campaign for him. Helpers work in the movement's Paris headquarters, known as QG (quartier general), and in local districts around France where they undertake a variety of tasks – from managing social media to leafleting, organising debates and events, going door-to-door and answering questions that come to En Marche via phone and email [...] Helpers who stay late or feel tired during the day can nap or sleep in a dedicated room of bunk beds. Enthusiastic Parisian teenagers without degrees or careers work on Macbooks and chat with the man who in a month's time could be president – Macron*

[135] *The Rise of 'Deep-Tech' is Boosting Paris's Startup Scene*. The Economist, 23 February 2016

[136] Lewis, Michael. *The New New Thing: A Silicon Valley Story*. WW Norton & Company, 1999

himself works on the floor above the helpers, popping down from time to time to mingle."[137]

Quite tellingly, the middle-aged champions of the French Gaullist right (François Fillon) and far-right (Marine Le Pen), both small-time lawyers with a scant grasp of basic financial economics, and the new left's leader (a grumpy Trotskyite typist turned Socialist school teacher) were all archetypal representatives of the old typographic-notarial classes. Their slow-moving supporters proved no match for En Marche's digitally choreographed electronic insurgency: *"every technology has its own ground rules, as it were. It decides all sorts of arrangements in other spheres [including politics]."*[138]

'And, At the Same Time' - and the New Radical Pragmatism

Macron's rivals on both sides of the aisle (from Socialist ex-friends to right-wing demagogues) often accuse him of being "an opportunist", an anti-centrist slur used by earlier generations of reactionary MPs... "The right" and "the left" are, after all, French inventions: it has thus never been easy to stand for the rational middle-ground in a Gallic political system characterised by a fondness for confrontational theatrics – "quarrelsome" is also a French word!

As if to provoke his critics, the new President has revived an ancient French expression: *"Et en même temps"*, which means something along the lines of "and, at the same time" or "and, on the other hand" – ultimately from *'autem'* and *'sed*

[137] *The Story of Emmanuel Macron - How an Ex-Investment Banker Became France's Best Hope*. The Irish News, 18 April 2017

[138] *The Future of Man in the Electric Age*. Marshall McLuhan Interview by Frank Kermode. BBC, 1965

etiam', Jerome's concise Latin renderings of intricate Judeo-Greek notions of 'dialectics.' [139]

Put simply, the *"Et en même temps"* principle means that, for socio-economic renewal to succeed, a modern, radical-positivist policy mix can only be rooted in the pragmatic centre of gravity of society as a whole.

This multidisciplinary, cross-cutting approach[140] makes for sound economic reforms: *"What happened last Sunday? [first round of the 2017 presidential election] French men and women have decided to close a long chapter in our history: they have said that the two main political parties [Socialists and Conservatives] that shared power for many years had lost touch with the people [...] As for me, I only have one enemy: France's fractures, its divisions. I reject notions such as the rich against the poor, the big city as opposed to the countryside, France's triumphant elites vs. the disenfranchises losers [...] I want to restore our unity to build, to create, so we can be proud of being French and European, of being ourselves, at last! "*[141]

---

[139] See notably Boyarin, Daniel. "Dialectic and divination in the Talmud." *The End of Dialogue in Antiquity* (2008): pp. 226 – 228 for an illuminating explanation of the major cultural-ideological shift taking place amongst both Greek-speaking (Athens, Antioch and Jerusalem) and Aramaic-speaking (Babylonia) intellectuals across the Roman Empire around the 4th century CE

[140] For the Neo-Comtian French *Positiviste* roots of much of modern socioeconomics, see Bell, Daniel. "Twelve modes of prediction: a preliminary sorting of approaches in the social sciences." *Daedalus* (1964): 845-880.

[141] Discours d'Emmanuel Macron à Arras 26 avril 2017
https://en-marche.fr/articles/discours/meeting-arras-emmanuel-macron-discours

IV

Getting the political back: the Podemos experience in Spain

by Antònia Casellas

nexpected in a period in which surveys provided evidence of a strong disaffection towards politics and the political, in Spring 2014, Podemos emerged into the Spanish political arena with five members elected to the European Parliament. This took place in a context of economic hardship in which Spain suffered from a growing and dramatic crisis of political confidence towards its institutions. Since then, and despite many efforts to discredit and attack it by consolidated political parties, Podemos has become recognised as a significant political actor within Spanish politics.

This essay first argues that the grassroots protests and general discontent that arose in Spain during the economic crisis together with the need to find a political alternative to the distrust of the population towards the traditional political parties, helped Podemos to emerge as a noteworthy political party in Spain.

Secondly, it emphasises that – despite the perception that there has been a shift from the political attitude towards an individualist moral attitude since the 1880s and a general depolarisation of society in the last decades – politics had persisted in people´s interests and has regained strength when a new party provided an alternative social and economic discourse to traditional political parties.

The platform: grassroots protesters or the germs of a new emancipatory political arrangement

Since the beginning of the crisis in 2007, grassroots protests in Mediterranean countries emerged as powerful demonstrations of citizens' discontent. In Spain, participation in street protests and demonstrations increased dramatically, growing in parallel to a significant decline in the confidence of the population in Spanish politicians and parties.

The 6th edition of the European Social Survey (ESS) (2013), a survey that collects information on the opinions and attitudes of European citizens, provided evidence of the strong disaffection of Spaniards, not only to politicians and political parties, but also to institutions in general. For the period 2011-2012, on a scale of 0 to 10, with a 1.9 average score, politicians and political parties garnered the lowest confidence levels in all items. The Spanish Parliament received only a 3.4 average grade, while the judicial system had a close score, with an average of 3.7.

The mistrust extended to international institutions, the United Nations, with a 4.7, was placed into question, while the European Parliament, having only a little more acceptance than the Spanish Parliament, scored 3.9.

The only institution which received approval in the 2011-2012 ESS survey in Spain was the police, with a 5.8 average score.

The results of this survey are significant, not only because of the low approval levels of Spaniards in relation to their politicians and institutions, but even more, because all scores were worse than in previous editions of the study.

Although historically in Spain there has been less confidence in institutions compared to northern European countries, the deterioration that the ESS survey revealed was remarkable. Economic hardship and the feeling that the system did not respond to the citizens' needs revitalised distrust and discontent in the country.

Nonetheless, concurrent to this phenomenon, Spaniards become gradually more active in street protests. Therefore, while the European average for participation in an authorised demonstration was 6.7 per cent for the period 2011-2012, in Spain, 25.8 per cent of respondents of the ESS survey claimed to have participated.

This activism suggested that, though it was evident that the country was suffering a crisis of political confidence, this phenomenon should not be confused with a worsening of political apathy. Interest in political matters increased during the crisis, and street protests demanding political and social improvements reached national and international media attention.

The origins of Podemos party ("we can" in English) relates to the *Indignados* (the outraged movement) (Hessel, 2011) movement as one of the most visible and powerful protest movements symbolising social discontent in the country.

Organized around a single claim, *Democracia Real Ya* (Real Democracy, Now) in 2011, the *Indignados* movement, also known as the 15M movement, appropriated symbolic urban space, in Lefevre´s terminology, for instance *Plaza del Sol* in Madrid and *Plaça Catalunya* in Barcelona. The highly visible struggle closely resonated with other massive political protests organized in other Mediterranean countries, especially the Arab Spring.

Nevertheless, despite the visibility and media coverage of the *Indignados*, when considering grassroots protests as a mechanism for political engagement and change, key questions arise. How could citizens' discontent evolve? Could this grassroots protest movement be an axis for social and political change? Can a leaderless movement be an alternative? Can they go beyond the momentum of street protest in order to foster institutional transformation? Could they become politically active and help to engender institutional regeneration?

The final answer was: yes.

The protest movements in Spain, fuelled by a critical economic situation, reintroduced political activism in the country and created the conditions for a new alternative ideological party to emerge, Podemos. A similar phenomenon to the one experienced by Ada Colau, one of the founders in February 2009 of the *Plataforma de Afectados por la Hipoteca* (PAH, or Platform for People Affected by the Mortgage) who moved from activist to mayor of Barcelona (Casellas and Sala, 2017). In June 2015, she became the first woman to hold the office as a leader of a new political grassroots party, *Barcelona en Comú*, in coalition with the Podemos party.

The resilience of the political attitude as a collective action

The French philosopher Comte-Sponville (2004) in his analysis of capitalism argues that, in Western societies, there was a shift of interest from a highly committed political attitude in the 1960s towards a growing moral attitude from the 1980s on. Following his argument, politics does not interest many people, especially not the younger ones. Nevertheless, in his opinion, this does not mean that young people are selfish and socially unaware. These same people, who have been massively disinterested in the political, shifted their interests and activism towards a significant number of moral concerns.

Comte-Sponville argues that moral concerns have often been renamed because the word "moral" is considered outdated. Consequently, people prefer to talk about human rights, humanitarianism and solidarity, which in fact encapsulates moral issues. The shift from the political to the moral meant that collective problems of a conflictive social and political nature were addressed through applying individual and moral responses, often under the umbrella of NGOs.

In parallel to the shift in the individual sphere from policy to moral focus, in the collective domain radical thinkers criticised the process of depoliticisation that institutionalised a series of new post-democratic governmental techniques.

Swyngedoew (2011), building on the work of Badiou (2008), Žižek, (1999) and Rancière (2004, 2006), pointed out that, in the last decades, a consensual mode of governance was created that has apparently reduced conflict and disagreement to either an ultra-politics of radical and violent disavowal, exclusion and containment or a para-political inclusion of different options on anything imaginable (as long as it does not question fundamentally the existing state of the neoliberal political-economic configuration) in arrangements of important participation and consensual "good" techno-managerial governance (Swyngedouw, 2011:370-271).

This point of analysis considers that politics at the empirical level became limited to conflict avoidance by repression when needed, or by the management of the commons. By reducing politics to policy making, politics apply an autocratic Governance-Beyond-the-State (Swyngedouw 2005).

In the analysis of this depoliticisation strategy, Rancière (2004) considers that politics in fact denotes inherent antagonism between competing representations of the commons. In this sense, he points out the need to distinguish, as Swyngedouw (2013) does, referring to the work of Paul Ricoeur (1965), between the notion of politics/le politique/the political on one hand; and on the other hand, the police order/la police/politics. While the latter refers to policy making arrangements of an everyday nature, the political is a more epistemological aspect which incorporates the heterogeneity that characterizes social life and, as such, it calls for the contested nature of the common. In this line of analysis, the protest movements, as Badiou (2012) asserts, represent a potential reawakening of the political, which could contain the germs of a new emancipatory political arrangement.

During the first years of the 2010s decade, political leaders and media confronted social activists in Spain with the argument that the state, or the political, was the arena to transform society. A few years later, the activists have proven them right.

The reawakening of the political in Spain took place in May 2014, when Podemos, a political parry created a few months earlier, became the fourth most voted party (7.98 per cent) in the Spanish elections to the European Parliament, with a list previously elaborated through open primary elections. A few months later, on 20 December 2015, at the elections for the national parliament, Podemos gained 21 per cent of the vote, becoming the third largest party in the Spanish parliament.

This experience and the subsequent Podemos victories at local elections provide evidence that the shift from the sphere of politics to the moral sphere and/or the depoliticisation of society have not won the final contest in Spain. The political attitude of Spanish citizens reemerged when people perceived a political alternative to customary politics; a tendency that has also taken place in other European countries.

In the December 2018 regional elections in Andalusia, VOX, a far-right political party that ran for the first time in the contest, captured 11 per cent of votes, with almost 400,000 votes. This meant that in Spain, for the first time since the country's return to democracy in 1975, a far-right party won seats in a parliament. Although *Adelante Andalucía*, a political left coalition that included candidates from Podemos party had close to 600,000 votes, the coalition lost was significant, as it went from its previous 32.6 to 16.18 per cent of total votes. This indicates that politics in Spain remain a contested and unpredictable arena in which traditional parties are not only contested from the left, but also, following a growing trend in European countries, from the right. A polarisation that may push traditional parties to establish unstable alliances with the new political parties.

References

Badiou, A. (2008). Live Badiou – Interview with Alain Badiou, Paris, December 200 in O. Feltham (ed). *Alain Badiou. Live Theory* (pp. 136-139). London: Continuum.

Badiou, A. (2012).*The Reawakening of History.* London: Verso.

Casellas, A. & Sala, E. 2017. "Home Eviction, Grassroots Organization and Citizen Empowerment in Spain" In Brickell, K., Fernandez, M. & Vasudevan, A. (eds.) *Geographies of Forced Eviction: Dispossession, Violence, Insecurity.* Palgrave Macmillan. p. 167-190. ISBN: 978-1-137-51127-0

Compte-Sponville, A. (2004). El capitalismo ¿Es moral? Barcelona: Ediciones Paidós Ibérica, S.A.

European Social Survey (ESS) (2013). (http://www.europeansocialsurvey.org/) [Accessed 9 December 2013]

Hessel, S. (2011). *Engagez-vous!* La Tour d'Aigues : Editions de l'Aube.

Rancière, J. (2004). Introducing Disagreement. *Angelaki. Journal of the Theoretical Humanities* 9 (3), 3-9.

Rancière, J. (2006). *Hatred of Democracy.* London: Verso.

Ricoeur, P. (1965). The Political Paradox. In P. Ricoeur (Ed). *History and Truth.* (pp. 247-270). Evanston: Northwestern University Press.

Swyngedouw, E. (2005). Governance Innovation and the Citizen: The Janus Face of Governance-beyond-the-state. *Urban Studies*, 42(11), 1- 16.

Swyngedouw, E. (2011). Interrogating post-democratization: Reclaiming egalitarian political spaces. *Political Geography* 30, 370-380.

Žižek, S. (2012). *The Year of Dreaming Dangerously.* London: Verso.

Also from Radix

"This is a book for this perilous moment; whether facing up to Brexit, populism or protectionism. Politicians, who have too often taken the inevitability of globalisation and the benefits of free trade for granted, need now to read this and think fresh thoughts, radical thoughts, about how to make trade again serve the public and our democracies, not overbear them."

The Rt Hon The Lord Lansley

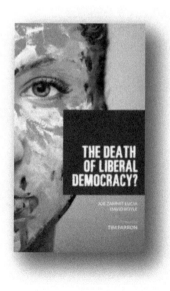

The authors argue for the current bland, politically correct, compromising centrist liberalism that comes across as weak-willed lack of conviction to be re-born as something clearer and fiercer. One that re-discovers its radical roots and is decisive in constructing an open society.

This book is for anyone, whatever their political party affiliation, who cares deeply about the revival of European liberal democracy in the face of an extremist challenge.

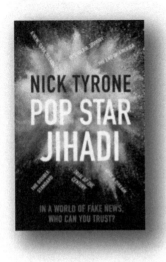

In this first novel ever published by a think tank, Nick Tyrone explores how, following a tragic event where a pop star blows himself up on stage, the social media narrative evolves so that nobody knows what is true and what is not. How, in a world dominated by social media and fake news, it is becoming impossible to develop shared narratives or even learn the truth.

"I would LOVE to introduce this book to a book club or group as a MUST READ."

Breakaway Reviewers

"This is an incredibly well written and intelligent piece of fiction."

Chloe Metzger
Book Reviewer

Also by Nick Silver

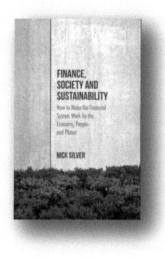

In this book, Nick Silver explores how we might be able to make the financial system work for the economy, people and the planet.

"Nick Silver challenges us to dig beneath the surface of finance and explore the fundamental changes we need to make if we're ever to answer the question, 'when will we know our financial system is working?'.

Professor Michael Mainelli

"An excellent and insightful analysis from an insider who cares that society is not getting what it deserves from the 'stewards' of its resources."

Professor Cynthia Williams

"Much effort has been expended since the 2008 crisis to prevent another collapse in the financial system. In this penetrating analysis of its pervasive failures, Nick Silver raises a far more terrifying prospect – that it survives in its current form."

Tony Greenham

Find out more about Radix

The think tank for the radical centre
www.radix.org.uk

Some of the Radix papers available on the web site:

What is the radical centre?

Freedom to Choose: Why competition policy affects us all

The Quadruple Helix: Tackling the issues of the left behind

A very British Brexit: A road map

Beyond Governance: An economy that works for everyone

What is the future of trade unionism in Britain?

Working Late: The importance of older women to our
economy

Quantitative Easing: The debate that never happened

Plus

Our daily opinion pieces

Our monthly Outlook newsletters on Globalisation and on
Competition Policy